D0580705

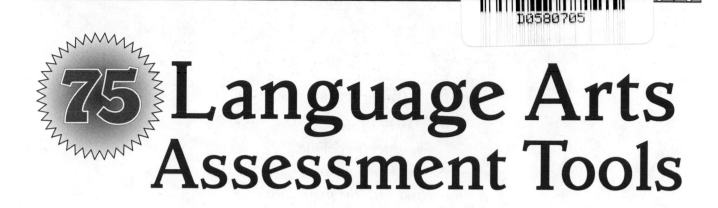

75 Language Arts Assessment Tools

Reproducible Rubrics, Checklists, Rating Sheets, Evaluation Forms, and More That Help You Assess Student Learning—and Plan Meaningful Instruction

by Mary Sullivan

NEW YORK • TORONTO • LONDON • AUCKLAND • SYDNEY
MEXICO CITY • NEW DELHI • HONG KONG • BUENOS AIRES

SCHOLASTIC
Teaching
Resources

DEDICATION

For Tom,
who encourages me,
and for Jo-Ann,
who helped with the manuscript.

ACKNOWLEDGMENTS

I wish to express appreciation to Scholastic Canada,
especially to Wendy Graham, for support in creating my early assessment materials
and for permission to use those materials in this publication.
As well, I am grateful to Arnold Publishing for permission to use my assessment
instruments published in The Teachers' Resource Package for Canada Revisited.
Thanks to Terry Cooper of Scholastic Inc. for her interest in this manuscript
and to Joanna Davis-Swing for her enthusiasm for the project,
as well as her advice and support in editing the manuscript.

Scholastic Inc. grants teachers permission to photocopy the reproducibles for personal classroom use.
No other part of this publication may be reproduced in whole or in part, or stored in a retrieval system,
or transmitted in any form or by any means, electronic, photocopying, recording or otherwise, without
written permission of the publisher. For information regarding permission, write to Scholastic Inc.,
557 Broadway, New York, NY 10012.

Cover design by James Sarfati
Cover photo by SODA
Interior design by Solutions by Design, Inc.

ISBN: 0-439-49158-4

Copyright © 2003 by Mary Sullivan
All rights reserved. Printed in the USA.

3 4 5 6 7 8 9 10   40   09 08 07 06 05

Table of Contents

About This Book

Being a teacher involves a great deal of record keeping. Schools and school districts certainly mandate an overwhelming amount of it; as teachers, we are required to gather test scores, statistics, and data of all kinds to measure and evaluate student performance and skills in the context of district-wide standards. And yet, many of these records do not seem to help us actually plan our teaching; they often seem to have little practical application within our own classrooms. Additionally, many of the assessment forms currently available are too general or too narrow for our specific needs. As a result, when we really do need to evaluate teaching and learning, we are often on our own in planning for, designing, and utilizing assessment forms that will actually benefit us and our students. That process is extremely time consuming—and as all teachers know, time is an extremely precious commodity.

The goal of this book, therefore, is to provide a fairly comprehensive collection of ideas, instruments, and forms that will assist you in planning and implementing assessment and evaluation in the area of language arts for grades 5 and up. And because the forms are varied and adaptable, they will prove useful whether your assessment is concerned with district standards or issues particular to your class. Some instruments are frameworks for gathering information about student knowledge, others provide criteria for evaluating student performances and work. Still others help assess student learning behaviors and attitudes. Some forms even invite feedback from peers or parents. There are rubrics for making global judgments and for evaluating specific tasks, and tools for assessing student collaboration skills and work habits. You will also find suggestions and guidelines to help you and your students create your own assessment materials.

You might opt to scan the information provided here as you create your own assessment plans, integrating the use of some of the instruments and activities provided in this guide with your own tests and checklists. You can also adapt some of the forms to suit your specific needs. Either way, many hours of creating specific assessment forms will be saved by using these ready-made instruments or by modifying them for use with specific assignments.

The Importance of Assessment and Evaluation to the Design of Learning

Assessment and evaluation are integral to the design of a learning environment. *Assessment* is the process of paying attention to something in a deliberate and purposeful way. It involves observing, measuring, describing, analyzing, and documenting. All of these activities can be carried out by teachers through general classroom observation and through specific observation of individual student performance. *Evaluation* is the process of making a judgment, and that judgment is inevitably arrived at through comparison. A student's performance, for instance, can be compared to an earlier performance, to a standard performance, to a specific set of criteria, or to the performance of others.

Assessment and evaluation *together* give us information about the level and nature of competencies, as well as insight into the attitudes and behaviors that support or inhibit learning. And the two main functions of assessment and evaluation are **diagnostic** and **celebratory.**

The Diagnostic Function

The diagnostic function is the single most important part of assessing learners, because the information we collect enables us to make sound judgments regarding our plans for instruction. Understanding learners' prior knowledge and skill levels equips us with ways to help every student enter the learning with dignity. This understanding guides us in designing the structures and supports that learners need to move forward in specific aspects of their development. And by showing us what learners can already do, the information we gain through assessment ensures that we acknowledge their competence by providing the challenge and enrichment they need.

In making a "diagnosis," it is important to realize that, behind the knowledge and skills demonstrated by students, there are contextual factors that powerfully influence their development. Students' confidence and motivation, willingness to take risks, tolerance for frustration, ability to focus, and levels of energy are all affected by their attitudes and experiences with learning. For this reason, it is as important for us to assess behaviors and attitudes as it is for us to document performance and knowledge. Instruments that solicit parental input can be of great value in gaining insight into these factors. And self-reports by learners about their own attitudes, interests, mental processes, habits, and activities also shed light on the unique challenges of individual learners.

As we gather more and more kinds of information about students' knowledge, skills, and attitudes, we can continually make adjustments and fine-tune instruction to give the maximum and most appropriate support to each learner. One student's frustration, another's excitement, and another's inappropriate behavior are all significant indicators in the teaching-learning dynamic. Feedback through assessment supplies the guiding light by which we can intervene in a meaningful way.

The Celebratory Function

A second compelling reason for assessment is to celebrate student growth and progress. As students see their movement along a continuum toward becoming literate persons, critical thinkers, articulate speakers, and adept problem solvers, they gain confidence in themselves as learners. They feel a sense of heightened control and empowerment. Truly, the "I can" experienced by a student whose success is made evident becomes the most powerful support to future learning.

Planning for Assessment and Evaluation

Learning is a profoundly complex dynamic, and the analysis of any aspect of it is a challenge. The broader the base we have for gathering information and perspectives on it, the more insight we will achieve into its intricacies. We are wise to solicit information about a learner or group of learners from colleagues, parents, and from the students themselves. We need to analyze artifacts, to collect samples over time, and to observe (both formally and informally) performances. We must also ask questions, observe and document, and give choices. For these reasons, many of the instruments and forms presented here are to be used by students themselves for self-evaluation, reflection, and guidance. These student forms complement the book's strong collection of teacher checklists and evaluation tools, peer evaluation instruments, and parent forms.

The Teacher's Role in Assessment and Evaluation

Based on the curriculum mandates for your grade and subject, you know the outcomes and standards your students are expected to meet. You also know the expectations for formal reporting to parents and your local jurisdiction. With these ends in sight, you must formulate a plan for gathering data to document the evaluative and descriptive information to be reported. In most cases, this includes evaluations in at least four categories: knowledge, skills, attitudes, and work habits (behaviors).

Along with your familiarity with curriculum mandates, you also know something about a student as a "reader." You learn this through performances (comprehension questions, discussion, level of reading material, and formal testing of literature knowledge), through habits observed, through what that student tells you, through what parents say, and through what the former teacher says. Having identified in advance what you need to know in order to determine a rubric level (or a grade) for that student, you would then decide how that data might be gathered. Forms in the "Planning Assessment and Evaluation" section (such as Assessment Planning, Targets & Goals, Creating a Rubric) will assist with such planning. Note that some tools include a "score," which is not meant to indicate a level of performance in terms of a "grade," but to reflect a sense of how students respond to a particular task, to provide a basis for comparison, and to determine if there is any change in response over time.

Designing a workable plan that includes a calendar for assessment and evaluation will ensure that you acquire rich data for effective instructional decision-making and defensible judgments for reporting purposes. To that end, this book features an Assessment Planning Calendar form. And in the "Assessment and Evaluation of Reading" section, you will find forms and instruments for collecting some of the information required to make global judgments and defend them with evidence. Again, these forms may be used "as is" or be modified to suit your particular teaching style, a particular task, and the specific needs of both you and your students.

Of course, many kinds of more specific information—information tied to particular texts, classroom content, and literature—must be captured in order to complete the picture. The Assessment Planning sheet will help with this planning by listing instruments to be used in the assessment process.

The Students' Role in Assessment and Evaluation

Students do better when they understand how evaluation works. They should have both the "big picture" of how the year's grade is determined, as well as specific information about the criteria that will be used for evaluation. Students should also always know the purpose and process by which their performance and work will be measured and judged.

Whenever possible, students should be directly involved in assessing and evaluating their work. Allowing students to help create the criteria for evaluation provides them with a heightened sense of control over their experience of the course content and over their personal performance. When students are consistently involved in the assessment process, they internalize aspects of evaluation and increasingly develop their skills in critical thinking and decision-making in other areas.

For instance, seeing the evaluation instrument for a particular piece of writing before they undertake the assignment allows students to see what it is they are attempting to do. Because this instrument describes the characteristics of a successful product, it can only assist students in producing such a piece of work.

The Parents' Role in Assessment and Evaluation

Parents also have a role in assessment and evaluation. Where their input can be solicited, parents often shed a great deal of light on how their children learn best. An ongoing open communication with parents will provide you with important feedback on their children's school experience.

Using This Book

The main areas, or strands, of Language Arts are covered in this book: reading, writing, listening and speaking, and representing and viewing. There are also sections on assessing group behaviors, rubrics and guidelines for evaluating, and even a section on how to plan for assessments. As you familiarize yourself with the Table of Contents, you'll see also that each of the main strands is divided into sections of assessment tools with a related focus. At the start of each section of instruments, a brief introduction makes suggestions for assessment planning for that particular skill area. This is followed by brief, descriptive paragraphs that explain the tools in that section—their functions, and how to use them.

Again, you might use many of the forms just as they are or integrate some of this material into your own assessment plans and forms, adapting some of the forms to suit your specific needs.

Finally, in addition to the many forms and instruments presented here, remember that the most valuable and critical factor is your own judgment about how, when, and what to use to discover the uniqueness of each learner.

Assessment Planning

The importance of assessment is clear. We understand the reasons for it, but we must also carefully plan when and how to do it. This section contains guides to aid in planning for assessment of various aspects of language arts, as well as several blank reproducibles that can help you plan and organize assessment in your own classroom.

Refer to the rubrics for each of the language arts strands (reading, writing, speaking, etc.) as you plan your evaluation for the year. Knowing ahead of time what global judgments you will be making at year-end about student performance will guide you in designing the content, processes, and materials students will experience in your course. Identifying appropriate activities/assignments will help you select and schedule the use of assessment methods and instruments in your unit plans. To that end, this section features an assessment calendar/schedule, rating response sheets, informal observation forms, and more.

Also included in this section are tools dealing with targets, goals, and accomplishments, as well as student reflection forms and parent feedback sheets. These rather "global reflections" will have bearing on the planning of instruction, on implications for review, and on recommendations in general.

Assessment Planning Sheet	Use this form, or some modification of it, to plan the instruments and activities you will use to assess and evaluate students with respect to the various curriculum outcomes dictated for their subject and grade level.
Assessment Planning Calendar	This calendar is a basic guide for planning and organization. List baseline assessment tools you will use in September, mid-year, and/or at the beginning of your curriculum units. Determine when you will use the rubrics and how you will gather information you need for reporting. An example of an annual calendar is provided (page 16).
Rating Responses	The Rating Responses tool records information about student work or performance to supplement the grades entered into your grade book. Use the Rating Responses sheet to assess your students' responses (spoken, written, illustrated, etc.) to any task. You might focus on one aspect at a time, though more than one can be considered.

In order to maintain records that will help you describe and evaluate student performance, you may want to name a piece of work, indicate the focus of the assessment for that assignment, and make brief notes about a particular aspect of the work. A numbering system (4, 3, 2, 1; 4 being the highest) is supplied in case you wish to make a global evaluation that will fit the rubrics for reporting (see the "About Rubrics" section). A sample of such a summary record is provided.

Note: the "scoring" system may vary for your district, which may use numbers, percentages, or letter grades to score performance.

Alternately, students can also use the Rating Responses tool to assess their own or their peers' responses to written or visual texts. Work with your students ahead of time to set up the sheet. Have them select two or three aspects to focus their assessment on and write criteria descriptors in the "notes" section. Then have them score responses.

Rating Responses

Name *Carlos*   Date *Dec. 3rd*

Title/Type of Piece *Descriptive Paragraph: "A Place of Peace"*

ASSESSMENT FOCUS				
Use of detail to support a main impression	(4)	3	2	1

Notes (scored 90%)
Carlos was able to create a strong image of his grandmother's house. The detail is rich and consistent in building the impression of this place as one of a comfort and serenity. As he describes the simplicity of the house and its tenants, one can imagine it vividly. This piece required major work on organization and mechanics but was very strong in the area of focus for assessment.

ASSESSMENT FOCUS	4	3	2	1

Notes

ASSESSMENT FOCUS	4	3	2	1

Notes

75 Language Arts Assessment Tools • Scholastic Teaching Resources

---

75 Language Arts Assessment Tools • Scholastic Teaching Resources

Informal Observation

Use the Informal Observation sheet to document any skills or behaviors you want to record informally throughout the year for individual students, group members, or the whole class. (See page 20 for a list of behaviors and their traits.)

This is a very versatile observation tool. You can use it to observe all students for a very general exhibition of behaviors. Or you may opt to observe individual students more closely for specific behaviors in a particular area of language arts. You might set up a sheet to record student behaviors as they are working through a unit, perhaps noting demonstrations of listening skills for literature circles, for example. Simply list the students down the side and the behaviors you want to watch for across the top. To observe an individual student, write in that student's name along with the behaviors you plan to observe. Then, make specific comments on the lines in the left column. You might also use the left column to note specific dates throughout the year on which you've observed that student for those behaviors. This will give you and the student a clear reference point for when you conference with them to discuss their independent work, and any changes or developments you've noticed.

This form allows you to document the language behaviors of particular students on a regular or intermittent basis. The data from this kind of informal observation is as important for your evaluation with rubrics as that gathered from more formal and deliberate tools.

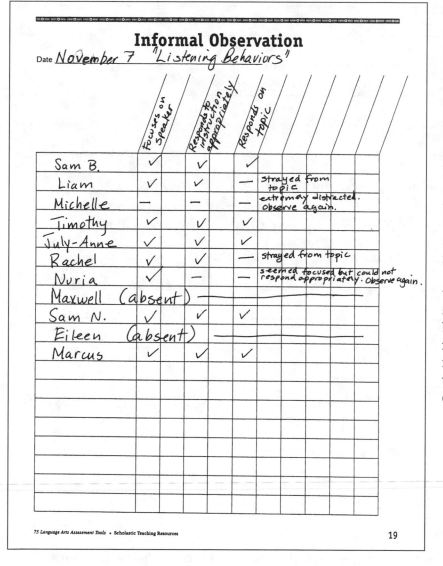

Assessment Planning Sheet

Term/Unit: _____

To collect information about students' understanding and application of concepts, I will use...
(Checklists for oral discussion, journal entries, specific assignments, critical thinking questions, student reflections, etc.)

(List assessment tool(s) to be used)

_____

_____

_____

_____

_____

_____

To collect information about students' ability to conduct research. I will use...
(List instruments that measure understanding of processes and strategies for conducting an aspect of research. List research projects, quizzes, self-reports, or peer evaluations that you will be using.)

_____

_____

_____

_____

_____

Ability to Communicate

In this term/unit, I will focus on the following communication skill(s):

_____ Reading _____ Representing _____ Speaking

_____ Listening _____ Writing _____ Viewing

For _____, I will use...
(List rubrics; specific work or performance instruments; self-reports that provide information about attitudes, behaviors, knowledge, or process; checklists; quizzes; activities; etc.)

_____

_____

(continued...)

75 Language Arts Assessment Tools • Scholastic Teaching Resources

(continued...)

_____

_____

_____

For _____, I will use…

_____

_____

_____

_____

For _____, I will use…

_____

_____

_____

_____

For _____, I will use…

_____

_____

_____

_____

For _____, I will use…

_____

_____

_____

_____

Assessment Planning Calendar

	SEPT.	OCT.	NOV.	DEC.	JAN.	FEB.	MARCH	APRIL	MAY	JUNE
	Use reading diagnostic tests, reading checklist, writing reflections, writing checklist, A Note From Home, Targets & Goals				Repeat baseline tools for comparison. Compare writing samples				Use baseline assessment tools to measure growth. Use student and parent reflections. A Final Note from Home. Goals & Accomplishments (Refer to original Targets & Goals. Goals & Accomplishments)	
	Use teacher-created tests and quizzes to test content and particular skills		Use observation checklists, anecdotal records, student self-reports to collect data on informal daily use of language, particularly of speaking and listening		Collect data from observations and self-assessments of group work and collaboration skills		Continue to collect data through observations, student self-assessments			
	Collect writing samples				Use unit tests, projects, products to assess student work.		Use unit tests to assess particular content knowledge		Collect writing samples	
	Use student work to assess product, knowledge of conventions, vocabulary				Refer to goals & targets to assess progress		Use student products, projects to assess student progress		Use all of the above artifacts, reflections, tests, final observations to create a global picture through the use of Rubrics to describe student performance in listening, speaking, reading, writing, representing, viewing	
			Use Rubrics for reporting on listening, speaking, reading, writing, representing, viewing			Use Rubrics to report on listening, speaking, writing, reading, representing, viewing				
	Notes: Early in term use baseline assessment tools for diagnostic purposes and to measure against later to demonstrate progress.				Notes: Mid-year repeat baseline assessment tools for comparison. Use generic instruments to collect data in an ongoing analysis of knowledge, skills and attitudes.				Notes: Year-end use Rubrics to summarize and present a global picture of student performance	

75 Language Arts Assessment Tools • Scholastic Teaching Resources

Assessment Planning Calendar

SEPT.	OCT.	NOV.	DEC.	JAN.	FEB.	MARCH	APRIL	MAY	JUNE

Rating Responses

Name _____ Date _____

Title/Type of Piece _____

ASSESSMENT FOCUS	4	3	2	1
Notes				

ASSESSMENT FOCUS	4	3	2	1
Notes				

ASSESSMENT FOCUS	4	3	2	1
Notes				

Informal Observation

Date _____

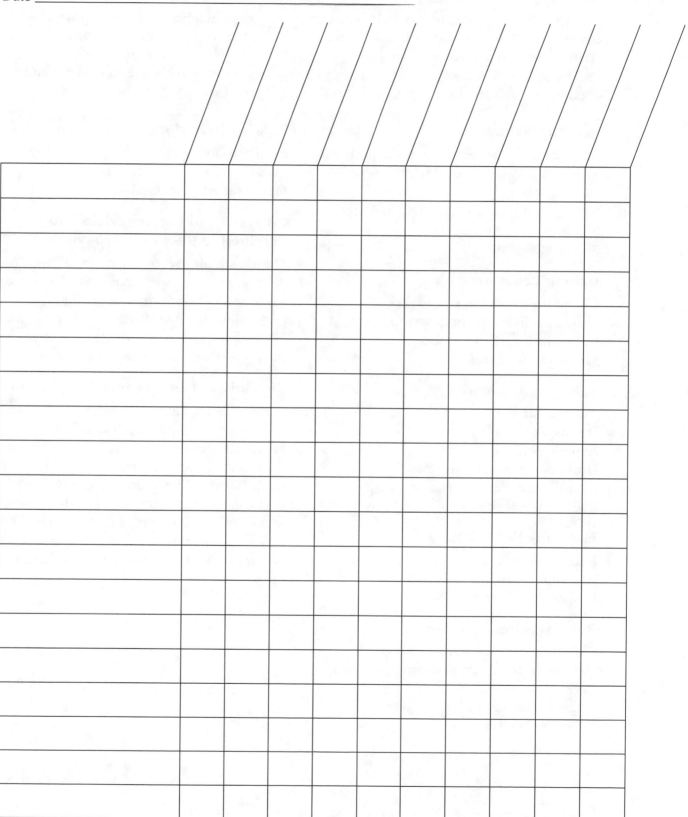

Using the Informal Observation Tool to Record Language Arts Behaviors

Since the observations you may wish to document need to support and give evidence of the summarizing remarks and evaluations you will make about student performance, it is wise to identify—from both the rubrics you use and the curriculum standards in your district—the behaviors that will demonstrate these competencies. With the Informal Observation tool, you can collect information that is not reflected fully by grades, artifacts, or other assessment means.

The following are some of the language behaviors you might choose to observe and document using the Informal Observation tool on page 19.

Reading Behaviors

Engages with the text (silent reading)
Reads by choice (reads during free time)
Discusses books
Extracts information quickly from text
Reads orally with fluency
Scans text easily

Writing Behaviors

Enters the task with confidence
Shows excitement about writing
Enters into revision process
Attends to feedback

Speaking Behaviors

Asks questions
Discusses ideas
Expresses needs
Uses conventional grammar
Speaks with clarity (articulation)
Uses wide vocabulary

Listening Behaviors

Focuses on speaker
Responds to instruction appropriately
Responds on topic

Representing Behaviors

Shows eagerness/interest in task
Demonstrates strategies for beginning
Shows preparedness for task
Engages purposefully
Uses time well

Viewing Behaviors

Focuses on activity
Asks questions
Makes reflective comments

Critical Thinking Behaviors and Conducting Research Behaviors

These will, for the most part, be shown in the literacy behaviors above. Student work, self-evaluations, and group evaluations by other instruments provided in this book will also provide data about these areas of student competency.

Checklists of Inappropriate Behaviors

In special circumstances, where there is a focus on reducing and eliminating behaviors that are barriers to learning, you may wish to create an observation list that identifies those behaviors to use with a particular student. Such a checklist might include things like *out of seat, talking out of turn, interfering with others, rudeness, playing with objects, refusing to engage in the task,* etc.

TOOLS & INSTRUCTIONS: Student & Parent Instruments

A Note From Home

An ongoing partnership with parents, both formal and informal, is essential to a productive teaching and learning environment. A letter from home at the start of the school year provides a formal opportunity to gather insights and information about the students in your class.

Summary Reflections From Home

Send this survey home toward the end of the school year. Parents'/guardians' responses will provide next year's teachers with helpful insights.

Looking Back
Student Reflections

Near the end of the year, have your students consider their accomplishments and unfinished business. Ask them to look over the samples of their work and the completed assessment tools in their assessment folders. Encourage them to discuss with a partner some areas of personal improvement and success. Once they have done this, have them fill in the Looking Back sheet. You might want to compare their responses with their parents' comments.

This activity provides an opportunity for students to crystallize some important aspects of their learning and bring closure to the work they have done over the year. Participate in their celebration!

Target and Goals

Identifying actions, habits, and people that can be supportive in achieving their goals is your students' first step toward success. At the start of the school year, discuss the Targets and Goals sheet in conference with students

---

Name _Jean_   Date _September 6_

Targets and Goals

* In my language arts program this year I hope to _write some science-fiction stories_

* One way I plan to reach that goal is _talk to both my science and language arts teachers for help and to see how I can work this into my grade_

* Something else I hope to do is _create a website and contact other young science-fiction writers and fans_

I have some expectations for myself this year.

* As a classmate I want to _add something interesting to discussions and projects this year_

* As a friend I plan to _widen my circle of friends a bit. Hang out with some new people._

* As a student I will _try to distinguish myself more with hard work and interesting ideas_

* As a group member I hope to _interest others in some of my hobbies – like science-fiction._

* Other comments _I know that last year some very good student work was published in the school magazine and I'd like to have one of my stories published this year_

26

75 Language Arts Assessment Tools • Scholastic Teaching Resources

---

Name _Ronald_   Date _September 10_

Targets and Goals

* In my language arts program this year I hope to _get a good grade and be a better speller_

* One way I plan to reach that goal is _do all my assignments and study the spelling words. Also to proofread my work._

* Something else I hope to do is _find some good books to read and do my projects on._

I have some expectations for myself this year.

* As a classmate I want to _have lots of friends_

* As a friend I plan to _do things we can all have fun doing_

* As a student I will _try to do my best and try to do all my assignments_

* As a group member I hope to _not goof around too much_

* Other comments _My brother told me he had fun in this class so I hope I do too_

26

75 Language Arts Assessment Tools • Scholastic Teaching Resources

---

before they write their responses. Have them refer to their filled-in sheet at various times during the year and fill it in again at the end of the year.

Goals and Accomplishments

The Goals and Accomplishments self-reflection sheet provides an opportunity for both you and students to review and assess their accomplishments as they relate to the goals they established for themselves early in the year or at the beginning of a unit. Once begun, the process can continually expand: As students determine what they have achieved, the following unit's goals might then be established on the basis of that reflection. Remember, though, that there should always be room to recognize both unanticipated learning and unexpected difficulties.

Name _Fiona_   Date _____

Goals and Accomplishments

✳ Name one personal goal you achieved during this unit and one you didn't achieve.

(did achieve) One goal was to get a good grade and I did.

(did not achieve) I wanted to find out more about forensic for my project, but never got around to doing an interview.

✳ In which skill area do you feel you have made progress in this unit: reading, writing, speaking, listening. Explain.

I feel I made progress in "planning" (I was more organized this time) and this did help a lot with the writing.

✳ Name one skill you plan to work on. Why does that skill need work? How will you work on it?

I felt uncomfortable trying to contact people to interview. I'll work on preparing myself better for that, maybe next time I'll actually get an interview.

✳ What have you learned in this unit about how you cope with difficulties or problems?

Well that I should have an alternative in case something doesn't work out (like my interview)

✳ What have you learned about yourself as a leader or participant?

Next time I do a partner project, I'll know that we need to sit down at the start to discuss the project and who should do what work, assign the tasks.

✳ How do you plan to show leadership and/or participation in your next group activity?

By being more willing to speak up about how the work is going and what we need to do to work well together

✳ What pleases you most about your performance in this unit?

I think the information and presentation stood out. We tried to make it look different and catchy, and it worked.

✳ Other thoughts about your work in this unit

I did learn a lot about my topic and about teamwork. I feel that I'm very prepared now for the next project.

A Note from Home

Your knowledge of your child can greatly assist me in meeting his or her needs. Please describe your child's interests, talents, and anything else you think I should know about your child on this form and return it to me so I can place it in his or her portfolio.

Your child's name _____ Date _____

Interests/preferences:

✦ Books, magazines, newspapers _____

_____

✦ Reading with you or with a sibling _____

_____

✦ Writing _____

_____

✦ When using the computer _____

_____

✦ School subjects and school activities _____

_____

✦ Hobbies and other general interests _____

_____

Also, please comment on:

✦ Your child's hopes and fears about school _____

_____

✦ His or her relationships with family members and friends _____

_____

✦ Your goals for your child's reading and writing this year _____

_____

✦ Any concerns/additional comments you have _____

_____

Summary Reflections from Home

Please fill in this questionnaire and return it to school. Your comments and observations will help me to reflect on your child's progress this year, and will assist next year's teacher.

Your child's name _____ Date _____

✸ What changes did you see in your son/daughter this year? _____

_____

_____

_____

✸ What new skills and accomplishments did you see? _____

_____

_____

_____

✸ What did your son/daughter enjoy about school this year? _____

_____

_____

_____

✸ What did he or she find challenging? _____

_____

_____

_____

✸ What concerns do you have about your child's experiences this year? _____

_____

_____

_____

If you have other comments, please use the back of this sheet.

Looking Back
Student Reflections

✶ As I look back over my work this year, I think _____

_____

✶ One of the best things about this year was _____

_____

_____

_____

✶ One thing that surprised me this year was _____

_____

_____

_____

✶ Of the literature we shared, the book or article I like best was _____

_____

because _____

_____

✶ One piece of work I did that I am especially proud of is _____

_____

because _____

_____

✶ One thing I still want to accomplish is _____

_____

_____

Targets and Goals

✸ In my language arts program this year I hope to _____

_____

_____

✸ One way I plan to reach that goal is _____

_____

_____

✸ Something else I hope to do is _____

_____

_____

I have some expectations for myself this year.

✸ As a classmate I want to _____

_____

✸ As a friend I plan to_____

_____

✸ As a student I will _____

_____

✸ As a group member I hope to _____

_____

✸ Other comments _____

_____

_____

_____

Goals and Accomplishments

✹ Name one personal goal you achieved during this unit and one you didn't achieve.

(did achieve) _____

_____

(did not achieve) _____

_____

✹ In which skill area do you feel you have made progress in this unit: reading, writing, speaking, or listening? Explain.

_____

_____

✹ Name one skill you plan to work on. Why does that skill need work? How will you work on it?

_____

_____

✹ What have you learned in this unit about how you cope with difficulties or problems?

_____

_____

✹ What have you learned about yourself as a leader or participant?

_____

_____

✹ How do you plan to show leadership and/or participation in your next group activity?

_____

_____

✹ What pleases you most about your performance in this unit?

_____

_____

✹ Other thoughts about your work in this unit

_____

_____

Assessment and Evaluation of Reading

Once students are beyond the elementary grades, depending upon their reading competencies and habits, we might classify them as non-readers, struggling readers, competent readers, or fluent readers. It is unfortunately true that some children beyond grade 5 cannot read; that is, they cannot make sense of the print they encounter daily. With these non-readers, you must still use the assessment measures and instruments designed for beginning and emergent readers. These types of early assessment instruments are outside the scope of this book, which deals with readers at a more sophisticated level.

However, it is still useful to assess all students' abilities to skim and scan, to locate information through knowledge of print clues and book parts. Walking students through a textbook's use of various print types and organizational structures is a worthwhile introductory exercise. Too often, we assume that students are familiar with the organization of textbook material when, in fact, no one has really explained what headings and sub-headings, indices, and glossaries are all about. These are new kinds of text symbols that students are being presented with as they leave the early grades.

In the area of reading, the focus of this book is to assist you in assessing reading comprehension, reading behaviors, and knowledge and understanding of literature. Some of the data can be gathered through observing readers as they interact with text and with each other in literature circles, in readers' workshop activities, in whole-class discussion, and in responses on comprehension tests.

Information about reading behaviors can be recorded using tools such as the Reading Reflections form (page 32) or the Reading Diagnostic form (page 34). These instruments, along with the Reading Checklist (page 33), for example, will provide data to support a global evaluation, such as those conveyed in the rubrics.

Instruments such as Reflecting on a Magazine Article (page 40) and Main Idea/Details (page 41) assist students in "mining" their experience with words and written material to practice reading strategies such as questioning, predicting, extending, and analyzing the text in more than a superficial manner. By using such instruments, you can gain insight into the depth of student processing and understanding of what they read.

The instruments dealing with literature provide information about students' knowledge of various genres, as well as their familiarity with story structure and the terminology to describe it. As in all of the assessment areas, the supports offered in this book are designed to supplement your own tests, quizzes, and response forms that relate directly to the literature and non-fiction materials of study. Rubrics on reading are provided to assist you in bringing all the information together in a summary evaluation of this aspect of language arts.

TOOLS & INSTRUCTIONS: Reading Behaviors

Reading Reflections

The responses on the Reading Reflections sheet will indicate a student's self-concept as a reader and his/her attitude toward reading. You can administer it at the beginning of the program, and again later to demonstrate changes in this important aspect of literacy development. You could also have students respond in a conference with you, or in their journals throughout the year.

Reading Checklist
Student Self-Report

The Reading Checklist provides information about your students' reading behaviors. It may be helpful to compare the information reported by the students to that gathered from the letters home to parents (page 23).

Name _Morgan_   Date _____

Reading Checklist
Student Self-Report

	Usually	Often	Sometimes	Seldom
I like someone to read to me	✕			
I like to read aloud to someone			✕	
I get so involved in a book that I can hardly put it down		✕		
I talk about books with my friends		✕		
I prefer to read books by my favorite authors			✕	
I read books more than once	✕			
I read books that were read to me by someone else	✕			
I like to read parts of the newspaper				✕
I like to read magazines			✕	
I like to read non-fiction, especially about ✱ sports ✱ animals ✱ science ✱ people (cats, I have a cat.)				
I like to read fantasy books		✕		
I like to read poetry			✕	
I know how to look things up ✱ in an encyclopedia ✱ in the dictionary ✱ on the Internet			✕	

Reading Diagnostic

The Reading Diagnostic tool can help you to identify, early in the year, students who may benefit from easier books and more directed teaching strategies. It can also direct you to students who may need specific one-on-one support, so you can collect the additional baseline data you need in order to set a plan in place for supporting and instructing them as appropriate. Discussion, observation, and direct inquiry will yield the information required here.

Reading Behaviors

Careful observation of students' behaviors at different stages of reading and during conferences can give you valuable insights into their level of comprehension of a text. The Reading Behaviors tool provides an extensive list of skills you can observe before, during, and after their reading. You may want to select a few items from each section, or concentrate on one section at a time. For example, you might focus on the before-reading comprehension skills for a few weeks, then the during-reading skills, and so on. You can complete this checklist several times during the year to monitor development of comprehension skills. Parent volunteers can also use the checklist to help them make appropriate observations when they work with individual students.

Name ______________________ Date ______________

Reading Reflections

* Do you think you are a good reader? What is a good reader?

* What is the best thing about reading?

* Is there anything you don't like about reading? Explain.

* What do you do if you don't understand something you read?

* What would you like to get better at as a reader?

Name _____ Date _____

Reading Checklist
Student Self-Report

	Usually	Often	Sometimes	Seldom
I like someone to read to me				
I like to read aloud to someone				
I get so involved in a book that I can hardly put it down				
I talk about books with my friends				
I prefer to read books by my favorite authors				
I read books more than once				
I read books that were read to me by someone else				
I like to read parts of the newspaper				
I like to read magazines				
I like to read non-fiction, especially about ✹ sports ✹ animals ✹ science ✹ people				
I like to read fantasy books				
I like to read poetry				
I know how to look things up ✹ in an encyclopedia ✹ in the dictionary ✹ on the Internet				

Reading Diagnostic

	Usually	Often	Sometimes	Seldom
Sees self as a good reader				
Enjoys being asked to read				
Reads comfortably and fluently				
Reads by choice				
Sees the purpose of reading				
Remains focused on reading				
Connects what is read to personal experience				
Predicts from experience				
Retells comfortably and accurately				
Has a good sight-word vocabulary				
Understands word families				
Uses reading strategies to find meaning of unknown words: ✳ reading ahead ✳ rereading ✳ substituting ✳ visual clues				

75 Language Arts Assessment Tools • Scholastic Teaching Resources

Name _____ Date _____

Reading Behaviors

	Usually	Often	Sometimes	Seldom
BEFORE READING				
Uses titles, pictures, captions, graphs, diagrams to make predictions				
Uses personal experience to make predictions				
Uses prior knowledge of topic to make predictions				
DURING THE READING				
Identifies when text does not make sense				
Uses prior text to make predictions				
Infers or reads between the lines				
Understands and uses the structure of the text to gain meaning				
Finds important facts and details				
Rereads when meaning is not gained				
Reads at appropriate rate for the text				
Is able to identify concepts, language or vocabulary that create obstacles to comprehension				
Searches efficiently for specific information				
Uses text to support statements and conclusions				
Distinguishes between fact and fiction				
Makes connections and relates text to other texts or media				
Relates and compares characters or situations to self or experiences				

Name _____ Date _____

(continued...)

	Usually	Often	Sometimes	Seldom
AFTER READING				
Reflects and extends comprehension through discussion				
Reflects and extends comprehension through writing and/or representing				
Identifies main idea				
Recalls important facts and details				
Summarizes main points				
Makes and justifies judgments				
Uses text to support statements and conclusions				
Identifies and explains author's message or intent				
Understands characterization				
Compares story characters				
Links story episodes				
Links facts in expository text				
Uses author's language in retelling				
Distinguishes between fact and fiction				
Makes connections and relates text to other texts or media				
Relates and compares characters or situations to self or experiences				
Interprets figurative language embedded in text				
Analyzes type, graphics, and illustrations				

75 Language Arts Assessment Tools • Scholastic Teaching Resources

TOOLS & INSTRUCTIONS: Processing and Understanding

Comparing and Evaluating

To assess your students' ability to recognize and evaluate the purpose and effect of different writing forms, ask them to compare two or three magazine articles they enjoyed reading. Instruct them, in groups or in individual conferences, to use the Comparing and Evaluating sheets to compare the selected articles under the headings Layout, Format, and Content. Then have students rank the articles from 1 on up, using 1 for the one they liked best. Ask them to give reasons for their rankings. Provide students with as many photocopies of this sheet as the number of articles they are considering.

Name _James_   Date _March 19th_

Comparing and Evaluating

Attach the magazine articles you have chosen. For two or more selections from a magazine, share your thoughts about:

✳ layout (appearance of the pages; photos, drawings, white space, color, etc.)
✳ format (effectiveness of form: poem, story, interview, etc.)
✳ content (most impressive, interesting or inspiring thing about the article)

Rank the selections (with #1 being the best, #2 the second best and so on). Comment on your reasons for making those rankings.

Title of Selection _CLUES TO THE PAST_

Layout _This article has an interesting layout because it has lots of color and space. It doesn't look crowded up. Each thing is sort of in a separate space_

Format _It is in alphabetical order so that is helpful and neat. The letter of the alphabet is in a blue jagged piece. The name of the thing is in large blue print and then there's a bit of information about it._

Content _I liked this article best because it had more facts than the other one. I learned more about ancient toys and musical instruments. I saw a picture of a vacuum cleaner that looked like a fire engine. I learned some new words too, like artifact and zither._

Ranking # _1_

Comment _THE BIRD OF PARADISE QUILT is cool because it shows the story of the bride's life. I think it would be interesting to dig things up and study about ancient times. This article makes you want to do that._

75 Language Arts Assessment Tools • Scholastic Teaching Resources   39

Name _James_   Date _March 19th_

Comparing and Evaluating

Attach the magazine articles you have chosen. For two or more selections from a magazine, share your thoughts about:

✳ layout (appearance of the pages; photos, drawings, white space, color, etc.)
✳ format (effectiveness of form: poem, story, interview, etc.)
✳ content (most impressive, interesting or inspiring thing about the article)

Rank the selections (with #1 being the best, #2 the second best and so on). Comment on your reasons for making those rankings.

Title of Selection _CAN PICTURES TALK ?_

Layout _The pages are not colorful because the picture the article talks about is black and white. But I like the way the information about the picture is in color-shaded boxes around the outside of the picture. Dots connect the box to the part of the picture it tells about. I think that's more interesting than just writing paragraphs below the picture_

Format _This is a good way to give the information. It's better to look at the picture and notice what the writer says about it. It's also really good to have the picture because you might not know what a pinafore is if you didn't have the picture to show it._

Content _I learned some things about olden day schools, clothes, and a little bit about photography back then, like it took a whole minute for the picture to be taken and everyone had to stay perfectly still for that whole time_

Ranking # _2_

Comment _I liked this article but I liked CLUES TO THE PAST better._

75 Language Arts Assessment Tools • Scholastic Teaching Resources   39

Reflecting on a Magazine Article

Assess students' ability to make supported judgments about magazine pieces by asking them to respond to all or part of the Reflecting on a Magazine Article form.

Main Idea/Details

Ask your students to use the Main Idea/Details sheet to identify main points (headings) and supporting details from an essay or article they have read. Assess their ability not only to divide the story into its main "chunks," but also to recognize the structure and its purpose.

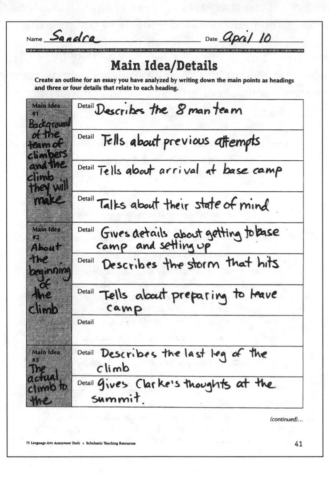

Name **Sandra**   Date **April 10**

Main Idea/Details

Create an outline for an essay you have analyzed by writing down the main points as headings and three or four details that relate to each heading.

Main Idea #1 Background of the team of climbers and the climb they will make	Detail Describes the 8 man team
	Detail Tells about previous attempts
	Detail Tells about arrival at base camp
	Detail Talks about their state of mind
Main Idea #2 About the beginning of the climb	Detail Gives details about getting to base camp and setting up
	Detail Describes the storm that hits
	Detail Tells about preparing to leave camp
	Detail
Main Idea #3 The actual climb to the	Detail Describes the last leg of the climb
	Detail Gives Clarke's thoughts at the summit.

(continued)...

75 Language Arts Assessment Tools • Scholastic Teaching Resources   41

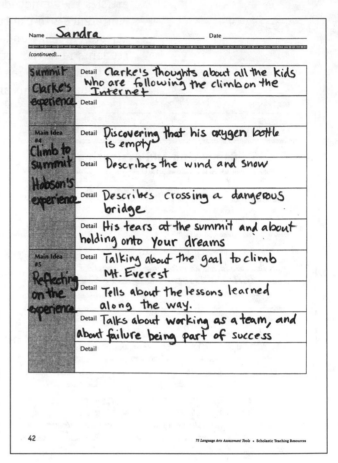

Name **Sandra**   Date ____

(continued)...

summit Clarke's experience	Detail Clarke's thoughts about all the kids who are following the climb on the Internet
	Detail
Main Idea #4 Climb to summit Hobson's experience	Detail Discovering that his oxygen bottle is empty
	Detail Describes the wind and snow
	Detail Describes crossing a dangerous bridge
	Detail His tears at the summit and about holding onto your dreams
Main Idea #5 Reflecting on the experience	Detail Talking about the goal to climb Mt. Everest
	Detail Tells about the lessons learned along the way.
	Detail Talks about working as a team, and about failure being part of success
	Detail

42   *75 Language Arts Assessment Tools • Scholastic Teaching Resources*

75 Language Arts Assessment Tools • Scholastic Teaching Resources

Name _____   Date _____

Comparing and Evaluating

Attach the magazine articles you have chosen. For two or more selections from a magazine, share your thoughts about:

  ✶ layout (appearance of the pages; photos, drawings, white space, color, etc.)

  ✶ format (effectiveness of form: poem, story, interview, etc.)

  ✶ content (most impressive, interesting or inspiring thing about the article)

Rank the selections (with #1 being the best, #2 the second best and so on). Comment on your reasons for making those rankings.

Title of Selection _____

Layout _____

_____

_____

_____

_____

Format _____

_____

_____

_____

_____

_____

Content _____

_____

_____

_____

_____

_____

Ranking # _____

Comment _____

_____

_____

Reflecting on a Magazine Article

✵ Choose your favorite selection from a magazine and tell why you liked it best. Don't just say, "It was great." Be specific about what you liked and why you enjoyed the article.

I liked _____ best because:

_____

_____

✵ Three new facts I learned from the magazine are:

a) _____

b) _____

c) _____

✵ Three things I would like to know more about are:

How the _____

_____

Why the _____

_____

If the _____

_____

✵ Two sources that might help me find that information are:

a) _____

b) _____

✵ I think that the purpose of the article is: _____

_____

_____

_____

75 Language Arts Assessment Tools • Scholastic Teaching Resources

Main Idea/Details

Create an outline for an essay you have analyzed by writing down the main points as headings and three or four details that relate to each heading.

Main Idea #1	Detail
	Detail
	Detail
	Detail
Main Idea #2	Detail
	Detail
	Detail
	Detail
Main Idea #3	Detail
	Detail

(continued…)

(continued...)

	Detail
	Detail
Main Idea #4	Detail
	Detail
	Detail
	Detail
Main Idea #5	Detail
	Detail
	Detail
	Detail

TOOLS & INSTRUCTIONS: Genre

Genre Clues
Making Inferences

Ask students to look at the table of contents of an anthology or a magazine and identify the genres included in there. Have them choose up to five selections (depending on your assessment needs) and predict what they expect to see as characteristics of those genres. Then ask them to browse through the book or magazine to confirm their predictions. Remind them to notice the headings, the way the pages are laid out, the types of visuals, and so on. All of these elements give clues about the genre.

Students should use the Genre Clues sheet to record their findings. Even reading very little, or not at all, students should be able to get some ideas about each selection. You can use their responses to assess their knowledge of genre characteristics.

Identifying Genres

Use the Identifying Genres form to collect information about your students' knowledge of a variety of genres. Ask them to try to complete the sheet in September or October so you have a baseline measure for comparison at the end of the year, when they can fill in the form again.

As students deal with other genres in the curriculum units, you can assess their understanding of those in the same way.

Name Lena   Date April 27

Identifying Genres

Describe the characteristics and give examples of the genres you know.

REPORT
Characteristics A report is factual. It can be written or oral. It has a purpose and a certain audience in mind.
Examples Weather report, an article on nutrition or on an Olympic athlete, a science report.

SURVEY
Characteristics Has questions. Records information about the person responding (male/female, age, city or town, etc.)
Examples School survey, a product survey, political survey, television program survey

INTERVIEW
Characteristics Questions and answers between two people
Examples Someone is interviewed for a police report after a car accident. A famous person is interviewed for television or a magazine.

REALISTIC STORY
Characteristics It seems real and could have happened. It's believable.
Examples Any of the story in our anthology — except the science fiction stories.

(continued)...

45

Name Lena   Date

(continued)...
Identifying Genres

SCRIPT
Characteristics A written form of speech. Dialogue written ahead of time, with directions about how to talk and move.
Examples A movie screenplay, a play for the stage or radio.

NEWSPAPER ARTICLE
Characteristics Gives facts and tells who/what/when/where/why.
Examples Information articles, but not editorials or book reviews.

NON-FICTION BOOK
Characteristics Gives facts and even instructions
Examples Books about gardening, books about records and music, books about WWII battles

BIOGRAPHY
Characteristics Tells about someone's life
Examples Life of a President, a sports hero, a famous musician or painter

(OTHER)
Characteristics

Examples

46

75 Language Arts Assessment Tools • Scholastic Teaching Resources

Note: More About Genres

Obviously there are genres not included on this Identifying Genres form that you may want to add or substitute depending on your curriculum. Some other possibilities might be: a poem, a journal or diary entry, a letter, a comic strip, etc.

Genre Clues

Making Inferences

For each selection you choose from the table of contents of an anthology or magazine, record the genre and what clues/features you think you will find for that genre. Then check the selection and record what features you did find. For your convenience, you may want to note down the page numbers.

Title	Genre	Pages	Features I Think I'll Find	Features I Found

Identifying Genres

Describe the characteristics and give examples of the genres you know.

REPORT

Characteristics _____

_____

Examples _____

_____

_____

SURVEY

Characteristics _____

_____

Examples _____

_____

_____

INTERVIEW

Characteristics _____

_____

Examples _____

_____

_____

REALISTIC STORY

Characteristics _____

_____

Examples _____

_____

_____

(continued...)

(continued...)

Identifying Genres

SCRIPT

Characteristics _____

_____

Examples _____

_____

NEWSPAPER ARTICLE

Characteristics _____

_____

Examples _____

_____

NON-FICTION BOOK

Characteristics _____

_____

Examples _____

_____

BIOGRAPHY

Characteristics _____

_____

Examples _____

_____

(OTHER) _____

Characteristics _____

_____

Examples _____

_____

75 Language Arts Assessment Tools • Scholastic Teaching Resources

TOOLS & INSTRUCTIONS: Story Structure

Story Elements

This form is designed to capture information about students' knowledge of story elements. The relative sophistication of readers will be evident from their responses.

Understanding Setting

Use this form if you want to assess students' understanding of setting as a story element. Individually or in groups, students can use the questions to reflect on the setting of a story they have read. Have students discuss the reasons for a writer choosing a particular place and time.

Making Inferences

Assess students' ability to make inferences by selecting clues and asking them to suggest at least one possible inference they can make from those clues. (You may select clues yourself or together with students.) Remind them that in order to "read between the lines," they need to consider not only the story clues, but also what they know about people in general and about the story characters. They may need to refresh their memory about what is going on in that part of the book. The Making Inferences sheet can be used for student practice as well as for assessment purposes.

Name __Cammie__   Date _____

Making Inferences

Combine what you already know with the story clues below to "read between the lines." What inferences do you make?

Title of book or article ___Lone Wolf___

Story Clue	What I Know	My Inferences
I walked home kicking every mushroom I could find	Perry was hoping a boy his age would move into the empty house	When he saw all girls get out of the car he was mad that there were no boys in the family.
"You're a great artist" she said. I felt my face turn red.	Perry is embarrassed that Willow has seen his paintings and he doesn't know what to say or do when she says he's a good artist	I think Perry is kind of happy and proud, but mad at the same time because she found his cave. It was a private place
Suddenly I was sick of her zillion questions... "I have to go now."	Perry moved there because his mom and dad split up	Willow's question about why he moved there upsets him. He doesn't want to think about it or talk about it.

75 Language Arts Assessment Tools • Scholastic Teaching Resources   51

Learning About Characters

In conjunction with the study of short stories or novels, have students use the Learning About Characters sheet to practice the skill of analyzing how authors reveal what their characters are like. You can also use their responses to help you assess their understanding of the concept of characterization.

Why Characters Do What They Do

Use this form to assesses students' understanding of character motivation and how the author reveals it, based on their book discussions and your directed teaching.

Plot Elements

Students select events from a story they have read and categorize those events in the boxes provided. It may help to do this together first, using a story read by the class or known to all students (a fairytale, for example) to show students the various aspects of plot and ensure that they understand the task. As an option, you may want to have students work together to come up with a "definition" of each element.

Point of View

Use this form to assess students' recognition of how the first-person point of view helps them to understand the main character's attitude, motivation, and mood. Literature allows us to look at things through the eyes of people different from ourselves. Ask students to identify a situation in a story or novel and analyze the perspectives of two different characters involved in the situation. This activity will give you some insight into the ability of students to appreciate points of view.

Name __Malcolm__   Date _____

Point of View

For each situation, describe the different points of view of two characters. Name the characters.

Situation	Name Willow	Name Perry
Willow intrudes in Perry's secret cave	Willow is surprised at first, then glad to discover the cave and Perry. She hopes they will become friends	Perry is furious that his cave has been found, especially by a girl! He doesn't want to share it or become friends with this girl.
Situation Brenda hears the remark Jamie makes and looks at him with blazing eyes before she runs down the hallway	**Name** Brenda — Brenda thinks Jamie means she should mind her own business and she is hurt.	**Name** Jamie — Jamie doesn't want to have Brenda in danger. And he also thinks she reacted that way because of what his father did to her family
Situation	**Name** _____	**Name** _____

75 Language Arts Assessment Tools • Scholastic Teaching Resources   55

---

75 Language Arts Assessment Tools • Scholastic Teaching Resources

Name _____ Date _____

Story Elements

✴ Story title (one you are very familiar with): _____

✴ Describe the *setting* of the story: _____

_____

_____

_____

_____

✴ Describe the *main character(s)*: _____

_____

_____

_____

_____

✴ Explain the *problem*, showing what the *conflict* is: _____

_____

_____

_____

_____

✴ List the main *plot* events: _____

_____

_____

_____

_____

✴ Tell the *solution* or *outcome* of the story: _____

_____

_____

_____

_____

Name _____ Date _____

Understanding Setting

✦ Why was the setting important to the unfolding of the story? How was the setting unique?

_____

_____

_____

_____

_____

✦ Did the author need some specialized knowledge to create the setting? Explain.

_____

_____

_____

_____

_____

✦ Was there more than one main setting? If so, explain.

_____

_____

_____

_____

_____

✦ What appealed to you most about the setting? Why?

_____

_____

_____

_____

_____

Name _____   Date _____

Making Inferences

Combine what you already know with the story clues below to "read between the lines." What inferences do you make?

Title of book or article _____

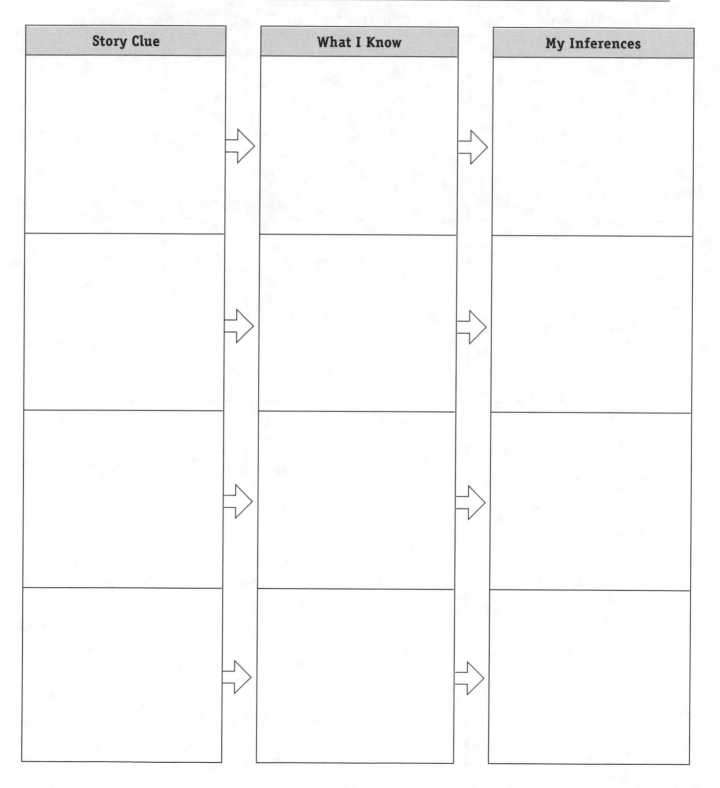

Story Clue		What I Know		My Inferences
	⇨		⇨	
	⇨		⇨	
	⇨		⇨	
	⇨		⇨	

Learning About Characters

Name the character, identify some of his or her character traits, and tell how you know those things about the character by listing clues the author gives (what the character says or does, etc.).

Character	Character Traits	How I Know

Why Characters Do What They Do

Name a character, select some things he/she says or does, explain what you think the motives for those words and actions are, and tell what you know about the character as a result.

What He/She Says or Does	Motive	What It Shows
Name: _____		
Name: _____		
Name: _____		
Name: _____		

Plot Elements

Element	Event	Why I Placed It in This Category
Introduction		
Set-in-motion events		
Complications		
Climax		
Resolution		

Point of View

For each situation, describe the different points of view of two characters. Name the characters.

Situation	Name _____	Name _____
Situation		
Situation		
Situation		

Assessment and Evaluation of Writing

The assessment and evaluation of writing is broad and complex. Within that broad scope, teachers are interested in **attitudes**, **knowledge**, **processes**, and **products**. We know that much about learning is connected to attitudes that students have towards themselves as learners in a specific area. *If, as a learner, for example, my experience with writing has shown me that writing is a valuable skill, that it empowers me to influence others and to share my ideas, then I will approach the task willingly. Additionally, if I perceive that my skill level and the support I receive will facilitate my success in writing ventures, I will approach the activity with confidence.*

We also know that motivation arises from such positive mindsets, and that motivation is a critical factor in student engagement and successful learning. For these reasons, it is important that we know something about the attitudes students have toward writing and toward themselves as writers. The instruments contained in this section that ask students to reflect upon themselves as writers will give you some of the information you need to gauge their experience and confidence as writers.

If students have had few opportunities to see writing as something powerful and important, they are unlikely to approach it with enthusiasm. If, on the other hand, they have had some of their work published, their letters actually mailed and responded to, or their note-taking serve them well for study purposes, they will be eager to strengthen themselves and express themselves as writers. Many of the instruments in this section are designed to assist you in gathering information about your students' writing experiences. The Writing Reflections and Writing Checklist tools (see page 59) provide insight into a learner's attitudes and habits. Bear in mind, though, that for those most lacking in confidence and skill, there is a barrier to putting anything in writing—even their feelings or attitudes about it. Conducting an interview with these students will help provide you with information about their reluctance to write.

Knowledge about the variety of formats and purposes for writing differs considerably from one learner to the next. Students who read widely (and for a variety of purposes) obviously have greater knowledge in this area. Some of the instruments provided here will assist you in assessing student knowledge of genres and formats, whether it's narrative or descriptive writing, biography, fiction, poetry, or editorial.

Knowledge of the conventions of language also varies from student to student. Although the first—and most critical—emphasis for young writers should be on content (on what they have to say), it is important to understand the degree to which student writers are inhibited by their lack of knowledge of conventions. In terms of instructional planning, it is also important to assess general student knowledge in this area so that you know which conventions you should teach to the whole class, and which you should teach only to those students who are working significantly below the level of the rest of the group. The Identifying Conventions and Understanding Conventions instruments (see page 86) will prove helpful in determining student knowledge of conventions, as will the students' own records of what they are working on to develop greater competence with language conventions.

There can be no doubt that writing as a **process** is the hardest area of writing to tackle, both from the point of view of the developing writer and from the viewpoint of the teacher attempting to coach writers in their development. If the collaboration between the "writer" and the "editor" progresses the way it ought to, the student will gradually internalize more and more of the necessary skills for reflecting on, revising, and strengthening a piece of work him/herself.

The coaching that results in such growth is an arduous collaboration—one in which the teacher accepts the challenge of attempting to mediate the student's expression of his/her message and one in which the student is open to critical feedback and encouragement to refine both that expression and the message.

Some of the information about this process of writing can be gained from having students reflect on the processes they are engaged in while they write. Again, the Writing Reflections and Checklist tools can assist you in discussing the process with student writers. The information you gain about how they approach writing may provide direction for instruction, and suggest activities for exploration and experimentation by student writers.

When it comes to evaluation of written **products** (pieces of work), the more the students know about the criteria for marking (what is expected), the more control they will have over their success. Having students participate in creating the evaluation rubrics is a powerful learning experience. Use the Evaluating a Summary criteria (page 68) as an example. This exercise can be done for any written assignment.

Students should always be given the criteria for assessment in advance of the assignment. Sometimes a checklist or tip sheet can be provided for them as their own guide to a first revision. Most of the checklist and rating scales in this book can be used (as they are or with slight modification) for self-evaluation, peer-evaluation, and/or teacher evaluation. Students can sharpen their ability to understand and use the criteria by judging the work of peers. (You can present this work anonymously or use examples from previous students.)

As students apply the assessment criteria to specific pieces of work, they increase their skills in editing and evaluating their own work. Having students reflect upon an earlier piece of their own work and solicit the responses of others to that work is also a valuable learning experience. Ask students to fill out a This Is My Work! sheet (page 64) throughout the year to facilitate this process. This instrument is also a terrific learning and motivation tool. Students should keep copies of all their written work and should be encouraged, at least once per term, to look at their areas of growth as well as their continuing challenges as writers. This can be one source of developing goals and targets for the next term. (See also Targets and Goals, page 26.)

Some of the instruments from this section, combined with teacher-developed forms of assessment, will provide the data necessary to make the global judgments expressed in rubrics.

TOOLS & INSTRUCTIONS: Writing Behaviors

Writing Reflections

The Writing Reflections tool will give you insight into your students' habits and attitudes about writing. It can be used as a one-time report to help you know where to begin with individual students, or for baseline and end-of-term comparisons. Reluctant writers will respond to this inventory more fully if you do it as an interview, or if their responses are written down by you or another scribe.

Writing Checklist

Used early in the year, the Writing Checklist will give you a baseline description of your students' awareness and use of writing strategies. Analyzing the responses of the whole class or of a particular group will also provide information you need to make instructional decisions about teaching the writing process.

This Is My Work!

Ask students to fill in and attach a This Is My Work! form to their work—not only writing, but any form of presentation—and then place it in their celebration or assessment portfolio.

Name Heather   Date May 9

This Is My Work!

Title and/or Description of Work Excerpts of Letters from Camp
Short Story

* What I like about it This is the first time I've written a story in a non-traditional format. Doing it as excerpts from letters was a good idea, especially since it saved me from having to write out all the descriptions and explanations that a regular story format would need

* Where I got my ideas I've gone to summer camp a lot, so I know all kinds of details about what it's like: the kids, the cabins, the activities, the food etc.

* What other people tell me about it Everyone who has read says it is great! Even my brother who usually has nothing nice to say read it and said it was really good.

* Teacher's comments Heather this is a beautiful story. It is moving and seems very real. The characters are believable and the dialogue is strong. The excerpts ring true. I would like your permission to share this piece with other classes. You should be proud of this.

* Parent's or other comments Heather's father and I are very proud of her story and we enjoyed it very much. She put a lot of time into writing it and revising it. She worked hard and it shows.

* Attachments (first draft, for example) _____
_____
_____

64   75 Language Arts Assessment Tools • Scholastic Teaching Resources

Rating a Writing Sample

Use the Rating a Writing Sample sheet, or a similar one you create to meet your specific assessment needs, to have students evaluate a sample of their own writing. It is even more effective to have a student or students work with you to develop the criteria. You might start with a simple rating scale in just one area and build on it.

Writing Reflections

✸ What kinds of writing do you most like to do? Why is that? _____

_____

_____

_____

✸ Where do you get your ideas for writing? _____

_____

_____

_____

✸ Is there anything about writing that you find hard to do? Why is that?

_____

_____

_____

✸ What revising and editing skills are you practicing?

_____

_____

_____

✸ How have you helped a classmate with his or her writing?

_____

_____

_____

Teacher Comments _____

_____

_____

_____

_____

Writing Checklist

	Usually	Often	Sometimes	Seldom
BEFORE WRITING				
I think a lot about my topic.				
I draw pictures.				
I think about the purpose of my writing.				
I think about who will read it.				
I talk to someone about my ideas for writing.				
I look at books or pictures to get ideas for writing.				
I imagine the situation I am writing about.				
I jot down words and phrases.				
I ask questions.				
I research information.				
WRITING A FIRST DRAFT				
I write as much as I can without stopping.				
I spell the best I can and keep writing.				
I read aloud what I have written.				
I ask others how my writing sounds so far.				
I put it aside for a little while before beginning to revise.				
I check out what other writers have done with the assignment.				

(continued...)

Writing Checklist

	Usually	Often	Sometimes	Seldom
REVISING				
I reread my draft to make sure it says what I want it to say.				
I read it out loud.				
I ask others to look at my work and suggest improvements.				
I cross things out or add things.				
I change the order of details or sentence structure.				
EDITING				
I check spelling, punctuation, and references to make sure they are correct.				
I change a word for a stronger synonym.				
I check to see that the verb tense is consistent.				
I rewrite a good copy of my work.				
If I am working on a computer, I try different font types and sizes.				
AFTER WRITING				
I share my work with others.				
I keep a copy of my work.				

Name _____ Date _____

This Is My Work!

Title and/or description of work _____

_____

✷ What I like about it _____

_____

_____

_____

✷ Where I got my ideas _____

_____

_____

_____

✷ What other people tell me about it _____

_____

_____

_____

✷ Teacher's comments _____

_____

_____

_____

✷ Parent's or other comments _____

_____

_____

_____

✷ List of attachments (first draft, research items, for example) _____

_____

_____

Name _____ Date _____

Rating a Writing Sample

Title of Sample _____

Rating Scale (Circle the number you think describes your work.)
4 = Excellent   3 = Good   2 = Satisfactory   1 = Needs Work

The content:				
✸ does what I wanted it to do	4	3	2	1
✸ has enough ideas and has good ideas	4	3	2	1
✸ gives supporting details (examples, evidence, description)	4	3	2	1
The structure:				
✸ is organized logically	4	3	2	1
✸ hangs together as a whole	4	3	2	1
✸ has an appropriate and correct format (letter, poem, etc.)	4	3	2	1
I have used correct:				
✸ spelling	4	3	2	1
✸ punctuation	4	3	2	1
✸ capitalization	4	3	2	1
✸ grammar	4	3	2	1
My work has:				
✸ a neat appearance	4	3	2	1
✸ special features (charts, drawings, graphs, title page)	4	3	2	1

TOTAL _____ (out of 48)

✸ What I like best about this work: _____

_____

✸ What I hope to do better next time: _____

_____

Evaluating a Summary
Student-Created Rubric

An important skill for students to have is the ability to make notes to record main ideas and details, and to create summaries from those notes. You may want to take the opportunity not only to assess students' ability to summarize, but also to work with them through the process of creating a rubric. (See "Creating a Summary Rubric," which follows on page 67.)

After you have worked through the process with the whole group, you can ask some or all of the students to repeat the process of creating rubric descriptors at appropriate times during the year.

Name _Trevor_   Date _____

Evaluating a Summary
Student-Created Rubric

For each of the elements necessary to make a summary, fill in the key words or phrases that would describe a "great" summary, a "good" one, an "okay" one, and a "not good enough" summary. Then, using the Student Self-Evaluation form, judge your own summary, according these standards, as "great," "good," "okay," or "not good enough" and explain why.

For a **great** summary, I would use the following descriptors:

Main Ideas _has all main ideas_

Details _has important details_

Order _things are in the right order_

Conventions _correct spelling and punctuation_

Appearance _Writing and appearance are neat_

Other _name and date are on it_

For a **good** summary, I would use the following descriptors:

Main Ideas _has most of the main ideas_

Details _has most of the important details_

Order _things are in the right order_

Conventions _spelling & punctuation are mostly correct_

Appearance _writing and appearance are neat_

Other _name and date are on it_

For a **okay** summary, I would use the following descriptors:

Main Ideas _Some main ideas are there_

Details _some details but not always the most important ones_

Order _occasionally out of order_

Conventions _there are spelling and punctuation mistakes_

Appearance _Writing is legible but is a bit messy_

Other _there are also some grammar errors_

For a **not good enough** summary, I would use the following descriptors:

Main Ideas _Missing important content ideas_

Details _lots of unimportant details not enough supporting details_

Order _mixed-up order_

Conventions _spelling mistakes missing and incorrect punctuation_

Appearance _messy, lots of cross-outs._

Other _grammar errors_

68

75 Language Arts Assessment Tools • Scholastic Teaching Resources

---

Name _Maria A._   Date _December 5_

Evaluating a Summary
Student Self-Reflection

Using the standards you identified in the student rubric "Evaluating a Summary," rate your own summary as "great," "good," "okay," or "not good enough" for each of the summary elements and explain your reasons for that rating.

✳ Main Ideas: _Okay_
I didn't have all the main ideas

✳ Details: _Okay_
I had some of the details, but some were not important. I missed some important ones

✳ Order: _okay_
I mixed the order up in one place

✳ Conventions: _good_
My spelling is good and I got my mom to check the punctuation with me. I only made 1 punctuation mistake.

✳ Appearance: _great_
I am a pretty neat writer and I copied it over to make sure it looked neat

✳ Other Comments: _good_
This was better than the last one I did

✳ Name 3 things you want to do better next time:
1. _Pay more attention to the important ideas_
2. _Talk it over with someone before I write it out_
3. _Read the article over and take notes on the order of things_

75 Language Arts Assessment Tools • Scholastic Teaching Resources

69

Creating a Summary Rubric

Point out to the class that, in order to create a rubric, they first have to consider exactly what is being evaluated, as they did for creating a rating scale. Ask them to answer the following questions and record their responses:

1. What is a summary and what does it include?

    (Main ideas, supporting details)

2. In addition to the content, what would it take to make a summary the *best possible* product it could be? How would you know that one summary was better than another?

    (Sensible order; correct spelling, grammar, and punctuation; neat, legible appearance.)

3. For each aspect of a summary you have listed, describe how it can be *great*. In groups or as partners, brainstorm ways in which a "good" summary and a "great" summary would be different. Use the Evaluating a Summary tool to list your descriptors.

    (Explain "descriptors" and work with the students to identify which of the descriptors they brainstorm can be combined or eliminated to reduce the list to essentials.)

4. Brainstorm again, and next to each "best" descriptor write an opposite one describing a summary that still needs lots of work.

    (Describing the extremes of success and failure makes it easier for students to build the rubric's in-between examples. It also spells out for them what they should try for and what they should avoid.)

5. Now add two more sets of descriptors that describe profiles that fall between the "best" and the "unsatisfactory." (This is the most difficult part. Students will need your assistance.)

To make the students aware of the rubric chart form you use, write the criteria out neatly on a blank rubric form (page 159), use it for rating their summaries, and then share it with them. Or invite the students to create the rubric chart and use it to evaluate their own work. If you have them create the chart, work through a sample with them first, as shown:

Summarizing			
HIGHEST LEVEL ⟶		⟶	**LOWEST LEVEL**
Main Ideas	*includes all main ideas in summary*	*includes most of the main ideas*	*includes just some of the main ideas*	*includes too few of the main ideas*

Evaluating a Summary
Student-Created Rubric

For each of the elements necessary to make a summary, fill in the key words or phrases that would describe a "great" summary, a "good" one, an "okay" one, and a "not good enough" summary. Then, using the Student Self-Evaluation form, judge your own summary, according to these standards, as "great," "good," "okay," or "not good enough" and explain why.

For a **great** summary, I would use the following descriptors: Main Ideas _____ Details _____ Order _____ Conventions _____ Appearance _____ Other _____	For a **good** summary, I would use the following descriptors: Main Ideas _____ Details _____ Order _____ Conventions _____ Appearance _____ Other _____
For an **okay** summary, I would use the following descriptors: Main Ideas _____ Details _____ Order _____ Conventions _____ Appearance _____ Other _____	For a **not good enough** summary, I would use the following descriptors: Main Ideas _____ Details _____ Order _____ Conventions _____ Appearance _____ Other _____

Evaluating a Summary
Student Self-Reflection

Using the standards you identified in the student rubric, "Evaluating a Summary," rate your own summary as "great," "good," "okay," or "not good enough" for each of the summary elements and explain your reasons for that rating.

✴ Main Ideas: _____

_____

_____

✴ Details: _____

_____

_____

✴ Order: _____

_____

_____

✴ Conventions: _____

_____

_____

✴ Appearance: _____

_____

_____

✴ Other Comments: _____

_____

✴ Name 3 things you want to do better next time:

1. _____

2. _____

3. _____

TOOLS & INSTRUCTIONS: Rating Different Types of Writing

Rating Narrative Writing

To assess your students' narrative writing skills, use the Rating Narrative Writing sheet. Choose a short piece of the student's work and assess his or her skill in this type of writing. The criteria included on the sheet are general. Space is left for you to add others more specific to your purposes.

Rating Descriptive Writing

Assess students' ability to write effective descriptive prose using the Rating Descriptive Writing scale as is, or by adding more specific criteria. You might want to modify the sheet to allow students to assess their own writing as well. Have students keep all their assignments with the evaluation sheet attached so that they can review their progress throughout the term.

Rating a Poem

Have students evaluate poems (their own and those of peers) using this tool. Give students examples of the various aspects of good poetry before they attempt to evaluate using these criteria.

Rating a Report

In addition to assessing the reports written by particular students, have students assess their own and each other's reports as well, using the Rating a Report sheet. The process of assessing a particular form of writing develops in students a heightened awareness of the characteristics of that form, and of ways they can improve their own use of it. Be sure to make the students aware of how your ratings differ from theirs, if they do.

Assessing a Story
Peer Assessment/
Self-Assessment

This tool encourages students to take an in-depth look at the structure and format of a story and to make critical comments about it. By assessing the work of their peers, students become more aware of their own mastery of a skill. Ask particular students to use the Assessing a Story sheet to respond to the stories created by their peers, and use their responses to assess their understanding of the criteria of a good story.

Before using this tool, it is helpful to review the criteria and model an assessment together with the class. Have students read a story and then discuss as a group the title, structure and plot, point of view, setting, characters and character development, and use of dialogue.

Name _Nancy_   Date _Feb. 19_

Assessing a Story
Peer Assessment/Self-Assessment
Tell what you think about these parts of the story.

Title _Plus or Minus a Few_   Writer _Jason_

Title The title is good because it is catchy. It also works in two ways. It's a saying but it also refers to what happens in the story.

Story Structure The story makes sense because it happens chronologically, the way the incident would have taken place.

Point of View He uses the 1st Person POV, which is good. It makes what's happening seem real. Since the 1st Person POV means he can know the character's thoughts, I think Jason should describe more what the character is feeling when he thinks about changing his grades.

Setting, Characters, Action There isn't much description of setting, but he could fix it by adding stuff about the commotion in the hall when the bell rings. Maybe some dialogue that gives you a better idea of who the kid is.

Plot The plot is very good. Lots of kids think about trying to change their report cards, especially when they were handwritten like in the past. It's harder now that its all done on computers. But I think he should struggle with it more. He decides too quickly.

Dialogue Some of the dialogue seems phony and some doesn't really add much to the story. That could be left out.

★ **My opinion of the story is** that it's good. You want to keep reading to find out how it ends. The dream part was a bit far out though. It might have been better if we didn't know for sure that it's a dream. We can tell for sure it is because parents would not act that way in real life.

76
                    75 Language Arts Assessment Tools • Scholastic Teaching Resources

Assessing a Letter as Literature

A creative project for students is to have them take the role of a person in history (a soldier in a war, a colonist, a fur trader, etc.) and write a letter from that individual's point of view. This form can be used to evaluate the product.

Rating a Review

Use the Rating a Review rating scale as is or adapt it as appropriate to assess students' ability to write an effective review.

Rating Narrative Writing

Rating Scale

4 = Excellent   3 = Good   2 = Satisfactory   1 = Needs Work

✬ The material is original.	4	3	2	1
✬ The writing shows logical organization.	4	3	2	1
✬ It moves at a good pace.	4	3	2	1
✬ Appropriate connectors hold the narrative together.	4	3	2	1
✬ The writing shows a consistent point of view.	4	3	2	1
✬ The narrative includes interesting details.	4	3	2	1
✬ It shows humor and suspense.	4	3	2	1
✬ The vocabulary is strong and effective.	4	3	2	1
✬ _____	4	3	2	1
✬ _____	4	3	2	1
✬ _____	4	3	2	1
✬ _____	4	3	2	1
✬ _____	4	3	2	1
✬ _____	4	3	2	1
✬ _____	4	3	2	1
✬ _____	4	3	2	1
✬ _____	4	3	2	1

TOTAL _____

75 Language Arts Assessment Tools • Scholastic Teaching Resources

Rating Descriptive Writing

Rating Scale
4 = Excellent   3 = Good   2 = Satisfactory   1 = Needs Work

The writing contains:				
✷ a single topic	4	3	2	1
✷ sufficient detail	4	3	2	1
✷ sensible order of detail	4	3	2	1
✷ precise and specific detail	4	3	2	1
✷ sensory detail	4	3	2	1
✷ figurative language	4	3	2	1
✷ strong vocabulary	4	3	2	1
✷ realism	4	3	2	1
✷ internal consistency	4	3	2	1
✷ _____	4	3	2	1
✷ _____	4	3	2	1
✷ _____	4	3	2	1
✷ _____	4	3	2	1
✷ _____	4	3	2	1
✷ _____	4	3	2	1
✷ _____	4	3	2	1

TOTAL _____

Rating a Poem

Rating Scale

4 = Excellent   **3 = Good**   **2 = Satisfactory**   **1 = Needs Work**

The poem titled _____

✦ creates sensory images	4	3	2	1
✦ uses figurative language	4	3	2	1
✦ establishes appropriate rhythm	4	3	2	1
✦ sets up an incident or idea	4	3	2	1
✦ creates a picture or a mood	4	3	2	1
✦ includes concise, vivid detail	4	3	2	1
✦ uses strong, precise vocabulary	4	3	2	1
✦ varies line length with a purpose	4	3	2	1
✦ _____	4	3	2	1
✦ _____	4	3	2	1
✦ _____	4	3	2	1
✦ _____	4	3	2	1
✦ _____	4	3	2	1
✦ _____	4	3	2	1
✦ _____	4	3	2	1
✦ _____	4	3	2	1

TOTAL _____

75 Language Arts Assessment Tools • Scholastic Teaching Resources

Name _____ Date _____

Rating a Report

Assign a score from 1–4 in each category, with 4 being the highest.

Introduction				
✸ gets the reader's attention	4	3	2	1
✸ describes who, what, why, where	4	3	2	1
Sections and Subheads				
✸ subheads help readers locate information	4	3	2	1
✸ subheads summarize the content	4	3	2	1
✸ information is accurate	4	3	2	1
Structure				
✸ has a clear organizational framework	4	3	2	1
✸ presents a logical sequence of ideas, information	4	3	2	1
Photos and Sidebars				
✸ visuals add interest	4	3	2	1
✸ captions explain more about the subject	4	3	2	1
✸ quotations in sidebars add interest	4	3	2	1
Conclusion				
✸ summarizes the report	4	3	2	1
✸ has a strong final statement	4	3	2	1
Overall Presentation				
✸ neat and attractive	4	3	2	1
✸ correct use of conventions	4	3	2	1
✸ error-free	4	3	2	1

TOTAL SCORE _____

Assessing a Story
Peer Assessment/Self-Assessment

Tell what you think about these parts of the story.

Title _____ Writer _____

Title	
Story Structure	
Point of View	
Setting, Characters, Action	
Plot	
Dialogue	

☆ My opinion of the story is _____

_____

_____

_____

Assessing a Letter as Literature

Activity _____

Consider the following and assign a score from 1–4 as follows:

    4 = definitely agree   **3 = mostly agree**   **2 = agree somewhat**   **1 = don't agree**

Discuss your scores or make your comments on the lines provided below.

✵ The letter has a purpose that is clear to the reader.   _____

✵ The letter is interesting and indicates details specific to time and place.   _____

✵ The letter shows that the writer has researched different aspects that are historically appropriate.   _____

✵ The voice behind the letter seems believable for the character.   _____

✵ The mechanics of the writing show good control of conventions of spelling, grammar, and punctuation.   _____

                                         TOTAL _____

General comments _____

_____

_____

_____

_____

_____

_____

_____

_____

_____

_____

Rating a Review

Title of Review _____

Consider the following and assign a score from 1–4 as follows:

4 = definitely agree   **3 = mostly agree**   **2 = agree somewhat**   **1 = don't agree**

The Review				
✸ expresses reviewer's thoughts clearly	4	3	2	1
✸ presents opinions forcefully	4	3	2	1
✸ hangs together coherently	4	3	2	1
✸ gives sufficient emphasis to main ideas	4	3	2	1
✸ uses relevant examples and details	4	3	2	1
✸ includes strong, interesting language	4	3	2	1
✸ uses appropriate tone	4	3	2	1
✸ uses first-person voice correctly	4	3	2	1
✸ follows correct writing conventions	4	3	2	1
✸ _____	4	3	2	1
✸ _____	4	3	2	1
✸ _____	4	3	2	1
✸ _____	4	3	2	1
✸ _____	4	3	2	1

TOTAL SCORE _____

75 Language Arts Assessment Tools • Scholastic Teaching Resources

TOOLS & INSTRUCTIONS: Biography and Autobiography

Profile/Character Sketch
Teacher-Created Rubric

This tool can be used in social studies or language arts to evaluate either a biographical profile or a character sketch. The items listed here are for a profile, but could be altered for a character sketch assignment.

Although this sample is a teacher-created rubric, it is always a good idea to involve students in a discussion about what things they must consider before beginning an assignment of their own or evaluating another's work. When you start a social studies or language arts unit that involves biography, ask students to consider the following questions. You may want to record their responses on the board in order to compare them later to the rubric you create for your students.

1. What is a biographical profile and what does it contain?

2. Imagine the best possible biographical profile. What, precisely, would it contain and how would it look? How would you know that one profile was better than another?

3. For each of the elements you listed for Question 1, describe what would make the profile "superior," "very good," "adequate," or "unsatisfactory."

NOTE: Before starting such an assignment, students need clear instructions regarding the length of the biography; the requirements for pictures, diagrams, and title page; and any other aspects of the task. These are, of course, the basis for the rubric you create and then share with students before they actually start the project. Depending upon those specifics, the rubric might look something like the sample provided below. For further suggestions regarding the creation of task-specific rubrics, refer to Creating a Rubric (page 157) in the "Rubrics" section.

Profile/Character Sketch
Teacher-Created Rubric

Use the following criteria to assess (and then revise) your work. Review again to determine if your final work is "superior," "very good," "adequate," or "unsatisfactory."

A *superior* profile:

a) Contains enough factual information about a person's life to provide background for an understanding of the person's achievements but not a great deal of irrelevant detail.

b) Focuses mainly on the achievements that made the person famous.

c) Explores the notion of the person's contribution in terms of his/her motivation and the characteristics the person possessed that made the achievement(s) possible.

d) Includes the relevance and importance of the person's contribution/achievement.

e) The profile is within length guidelines, and (if required) includes a correctly formatted bibliography.

A *very good* profile:

a) Contains enough factual information about a person's life to provide background for an understanding of the person's achievements but not a great deal of irrelevant detail.

b) Focuses mainly on the achievements that made the person famous.

c) Contains some mention of the person's contribution in terms of his/her motivation and the characteristics of the person that made the achievement(s) possible.

da) Includes some reference to the relevance and importance of the person's achievement.

b) The profile is within the length guidelines. If required, it contains a bibliography, though there may be some formatting errors.

An *adequate* profile:

a) May contain insufficient detail about the person's life for an understanding of the context of the person's accomplishment(s). May contain some irrelevant details.

b) Lacks strong focus on those achievements that made the person famous.

c) Provides little or no mention of the person's contribution(s) in terms of his/her motivation or the characteristics the person possessed that made the achievement(s) possible. d) Includes little or no reference to the relevance and importance of the person's contribution or achievement.

d) The profile is shorter (or significantly longer) than the guidelines specified. The bibliography (if required) is missing or contains a great number of formatting errors.

An *unsatisfactory* profile:

a) May contain insufficient detail about the person's life for an understanding of the context of the person's accomplishment(s). May contain a great deal of irrelevant details.

b) Does not particularly focus on those achievements that made the person famous.

c) Does not attempt to provide insight into the person's contribution(s) in terms of his/her motivation or the characteristics the person possessed that made the achievement(s) possible.

d) ncludes little or no reference to the relevance and importance of the person's contribution or achievement.

e) The profile is shorter than the guidelines specified. The bibliography (if required) is missing.

Profile/Character Sketch
Teacher-Created Rubric

Use the following criteria to assess (and then revise) your work. Review again to determine if your final work is "superior," "very good," "adequate," or "unsatisfactory."

A *superior* profile:

_____

_____

_____

_____

_____

_____

_____

_____

A *very good* profile:

_____

_____

_____

_____

_____

_____

An *adequate* profile:

_____

_____

_____

_____

_____

_____

_____

_____

An *unsatisfactory* profile:

_____

_____

_____

_____

_____

_____

Rating a Biographical Sketch

Using this form, students can assess their own or their classmates' writing of a biography. Use any or all of the questions to assess students' general knowledge of this form of writing, adding criteria to the sheet as appropriate for your purposes.

Rating a Profile
Biographical Sketch/
Character Sketch

The Rating a Profile sheet helps you assess the writing samples created by specific students. If appropriate, you can also use it to help students evaluate their own work. Add to or modify the criteria to meet your specific assessment needs.

Response to Your Autobiography

This descriptive assessment of student autobiographies reminds students of some important aspects of writing to share personal information, and offers comments about their success with these aspects. Use the reproducible provided, if it suits your needs, or create a similar list of comments for yourself.

Name _____ Date _____

Rating a Biographical Sketch

Rating Scale (Circle the number you think describes your work.)

4 = very well   3 = well   2 = satisfactorily   1 = not enough

✳ The biography shows why the person became famous.	4	3	2	1
✳ It gives details about how the person developed the particular interest that brought him or her fame.	4	3	2	1
✳ It describes the characteristics of the person that helped make him or her successful.	4	3	2	1
✳ The biography holds the reader's interest.	4	3	2	1
✳ It makes the reader want to know more about the person or the topic.	4	3	2	1
✳ The writing is clear and well organized.	4	3	2	1
✳ The information is accurate.	4	3	2	1
✳ The writer has attended to the conventions of spelling, grammar, and punctuation.	4	3	2	1
✳ The tone is appropriate for the intended audience.	4	3	2	1
✳ The writer has included interesting language, dialogue, humor, or examples.	4	3	2	1
✳ _____ _____	4	3	2	1
✳ _____ _____	4	3	2	1
✳ _____ _____	4	3	2	1

TOTAL SCORE _____

75 Language Arts Assessment Tools • Scholastic Teaching Resources

Rating a Profile
Biographical Sketch/Character Sketch

Circle the number that matches your opinion of these features of the profile. Use the following scale:

4 = excellent   3 = good   2 = satisfactory   1 = needs improvement

✹ The profile gives adequate information about the person/character.	4	3	2	1
✹ It provides interesting details about the person's/character's job, interests, accomplishments, etc.	4	3	2	1
✹ It uses strong, descriptive language.	4	3	2	1
✹ The profile leaves the reader wanting to know more about the person/character.	4	3	2	1
✹ The information is organized in a sensible order.	4	3	2	1
✹ The profile is neat and uses correct writing conventions.	4	3	2	1
✹ It includes photos/drawings or other visuals to add interest.	4	3	2	1
✹ _____ _____	4	3	2	1
✹ _____ _____	4	3	2	1
✹ _____ _____	4	3	2	1
✹ _____ _____	4	3	2	1

TOTAL SCORE _____

Response to Your Autobiography

Here are some comments on your autobiography and/or some suggestions you might think about.

✴ It is important to include personal details in an autobiography. Both the number and the kind of details are important. We think about and/or research those details during pre-writing activities. Having seen your pre-writing activities (discussions, webs, outlines, lists, drafts), I would say that…

_____

_____

_____

_____

✴ The ideas generated can be kind of ho-hum, just common, general information. Or they can be interesting and vivid. It depends on what and how the writer shares. I found your content…

_____

_____

_____

_____

✴ The organization of ideas—the sequence, the order, the clustering of details—makes the work more readable and gives it more emphasis. The organization of your autobiography seems…

_____

_____

_____

_____

✴ Sometimes the format chosen for sharing ideas is particularly effective. Some comments or suggestions about the format you chose for sharing your autobiography are…

_____

_____

_____

_____

(continued…)

(continued...)

Response to Your Autobiography

✦ The finishing touches a person puts on the work really say something about him or her and how he or she views the assignment. Finishing touches include revision and editing, as well as special features (pictures, captions, artwork). As a reader, looking at your finishing touches makes me think…

_____

_____

_____

✦ The overall presentation usually leaves the audience/reader with a main impression of the work. Sometimes the audience/reader responds to something specific instead. Your autobiography…

_____

_____

_____

_____

✦ Different things stand out for different people. The thing I like best about your autobiography is…

_____

_____

_____

_____

_____

_____

TOOLS & INSTRUCTIONS: Language Conventions

Language Conventions

The sample tools here will help you determine your students' understanding of the conventions they find in their reading and use in their writing. Adapt and use them to assess understanding of conventions in any passage of your choosing or in any of the students' own written work. You might find it helpful to work through this first sample exercise together with your students. (Note: 1 = comma; 2 = apostraphe; 3 = capitalization; 4 = comma; 5 = hyphen.)

Identifying Conventions

Choose any passage and assign a number to the conventions you want to assess, then ask students to record their responses on the Identifying Conventions sheet.

Understanding Conventions

Use the Understanding Conventions tool with individual students in conference to record their recognition and understanding of specific conventions. If you are using this tool as a baseline measurement of student understanding of conventions, administer it again later in the year to document the learning that has taken place.

If you are assessing individuals or small groups, you can tailor the assessment by asking more able students to respond to/identify more sophisticated conventions. Once you have worked through this activity with students one on one, they can do it with peer partners using any piece of prose. Use the same passage each time.

Having students do these activities orally will make you aware of what vocabulary they possess for describing conventions. This in turn gives you an opportunity to teach and encourage precise language in referring to specific conventions. It will also give you more insight into students' knowledge of these concepts and their ability to use the conventions as cues to meaning.

Many students understand conventions much better than their written work indicates. Often, errors and omissions result more from laziness or lack of pride in accomplishment than from lack of knowledge or understanding. If this is the case, you may need to revise your instructional strategies for particular students.

NOTE: Another approach to assessing an understanding of conventions is to ask students to search through a text to locate examples of conventions themselves, identifying and explaining them. This will also be helpful in determining which conventions should be reinforced for the whole class and which should be reinforced for individual students.

75 Language Arts Assessment Tools • Scholastic Teaching Resources

Language Conventions

When we speak, our tone of voice, pauses, and emphasis help to make our meaning clear. But these are absent from written language, so we use special visual clues that help our readers understand us when we write—clues like spaces, punctuation, and spelling. We respond to these signals every time we read.

You already use many of these "conventions" in your own writing. Some of the more complicated ones you may not always use correctly yet, even if you understand them. The Identifying Conventions sheets will help you to see what you know about writing conventions. Read the passage your teacher gives you and name each convention marked with a number. Explain why these conventions are used as they are and where they are. Here is an example:

1   2   3
Mike, Ryan's father, has always been there to support him. In

4   5
1996, Mike suggested that the two of them make a cross-country
bike tour to raise money for the physically challenged.

	Name of Convention	**What It Does**
1		
2		
3		
4		
5		

Identifying Conventions

	Name of Convention	What it Does
1		
2		
3		
4		
5		
6		
7		
8		
9		
10		
11		
12		
13		
14		
15		
16		
17		
18		

75 Language Arts Assessment Tools • Scholastic Teaching Resources

Name _____ Date _____

Understanding Conventions

Text Used: _____

	Convention	Names Correctly	Knows Purpose
1	Capital letter to begin a sentence or quote		
2	Capital letter for names and titles		
3	Period ending sentences		
4	Period for abbreviations		
5	Question mark		
6	Exclamation mark		
7	Comma in a series		
8	Comma to set off dates and places		
9	Comma to set off the speaker in dialogue		
10	Comma to set off introductory words		
11	Comma to set off explanatory words		
12	Comma to separate main clauses		
13	Quotation marks in dialogue		
14	Quotation marks around direct quotes		
15	Quotation marks around titles		
16	Apostrophe showing possession		
17	Apostrophe in contractions		
18	Colon before a list		
19	Dash to show break in thought or words		
20	Dash for emphasis		
21	Ellipsis to indicate missing words		
22	Hyphen in compound words		
23	Paragraphs in dialogue		
24	Italic or bold for emphasis		
25	Italic to highlight specific words		

TOOLS & INSTRUCTIONS: Note-Taking Skills

Note-Taking Self-Evaluation	This instrument provides some structure for students wishing to assess their subject notes. Note-taking can be critical to the learning process. Students who test/perform poorly often lack focus and structure in their subject notes. However, taking good notes is a real skill—one that can be learned and assessed. You might wish to create a rubric together with your students that describes criteria for good notes. Suggestions for creating rubrics with students are found in the student self-evaluation Note-Taking form. This process could be adapted to the creation of rubrics for note-taking.
Teacher Rating of Note-Taking Skills	Periodically collect students' notes from a note-taking activity (perhaps once every other chapter) and evaluate them individually using the rating scale.

Note-Taking
Self-Evaluation

At the end of each chapter of study, take time to glance through your notes and your work to assess and organize your notebook. A careful and complete record of classroom discussions and activities will make review easier and more worthwhile. Keeping all of your quizzes and assignments will help you analyze and identify those areas that require more attention. Look at your notes in light of the following criteria and decide how you can better support your learning by making some changes in your note-taking.

Look at *What* You Record

✷ How do your notes demonstrate that you have tried to keep a complete record of the material studied?

_____

_____

_____

✷ What strategies do you use for collecting material and information you might have missed due to an absence or a lack of understanding?

_____

_____

_____

Look at *How* You Record

✷ Are your notes neat and legible? _____

If not, how can they be improved? _____

✷ Are your separate notes, assignments, and activities organized in such a way that they are easy to locate?

_____

_____

If not, what strategy would help you to ensure that your notes are managed better?

_____

_____

✷ Are your title pages and visual representations clear and interesting?

_____

_____

(continued...)

(continued...)

Note-Taking

Think About How You *Use* Your Notes

☆ How often do you read through your notes? _____

_____

_____

_____

☆ How often do you check with a classmate to compare notes? _____

_____

_____

_____

☆ How do you use your notes, assignments, and past quizzes to prepare for exams?

_____

_____

_____

_____

☆ How do you use the information in your notes to help generate ideas for assignments?

_____

_____

_____

_____

Name _____ Date _____

Teacher Rating of Note-Taking Skills

Activity _____ Class _____

4 = excellent   3 = good   2 = satisfactory   1 = needs improvement

✧ Student's notes provide sufficient detail.	4	3	2	1
✧ Student's notes highlight only important information.	4	3	2	1
✧ Information in student's notes is organized.	4	3	2	1
✧ Student's notes were in point form.	4	3	2	1
✧ Student's notes are organized by headings/subheadings.	4	3	2	1
✧ Student's notes are legible.	4	3	2	1

General comments _____

_____

_____

_____

_____

_____

_____

_____

_____

_____

Assessment and Evaluation of Listening and Speaking

As teachers, we want to know something about students' competencies and behaviors in the areas of listening and speaking. A student who is inattentive may do poorly when asked to report on what has been presented by you or by another speaker. The same student may score very high on tests of listening skills if, in fact, he or she is motivated to do so. And, of course, another student may listen well in low-risk settings, but "freeze up" in a quiz that attempts to measure his or her ability to follow directions. The Listening Quiz (pages 100–101) is an open-ended instrument that will help you assess listening skills. This tool enables you to supply detailed directions in as simple or complex a form as is suitable to your students and your purposes.

If there is a significant discrepancy between a student's typical listening patterns in the low-risk situations and more high-risk or formal evaluations, this should be investigated. The lack of focus and attentiveness in either context can have an affective cause apart from other factors. For such circumstances, the Oral Presentation: Listening Critically tool (page 98) allows students to show how well they can take in information presented orally, and also calls for critical thinking in terms of inference and evaluation.

In informal circumstances, communication patterns indicate preferences and personal styles, in addition to competencies. It is important to provide small group and paired discussion opportunities since not all students are comfortable with sharing in a large group, even though they may be competent with the material and confident in their ideas. It is also important to have learners tell us about those preferred styles of sharing knowledge and making contributions. Speaking Checklist: Student Self-Report (page 103) is useful for this.

A strong practice for the development of formal speaking competencies is to involve students regularly in peer-assessment and self-assessment against criteria. Instruments such as Rating an Oral Presentation (page 106) and Rating Storytelling (page 107) serve such a purpose.

Finally, as with the assessment and evaluation of all skills, it is important for teachers to observe learners in collaboration and in discussion to gather information about speaking and listening competencies. In this regard, the instruments that deal with student participation in group processing and collaboration will be useful as well. (See the "Group Work and Participation" section, page 137.)

TOOLS & INSTRUCTIONS: Listening

Oral Presentation: Listening Critically

Students need to become aware of the criteria for judging the quality of a presentation. After you have thoroughly discussed particular criteria, you can assess individual students' grasp of what is required by monitoring their presentations using the Oral Presentation sheets. The sheets are set up for student responses if you want them to assess their own or each other's presentations. However, you should select only two or three questions for students to respond to at one time. The process of assessing the speeches of peers develops in students a heightened awareness of all that goes into a good speech, and of ways they can improve their own presentations.

Listening Quiz

You can assess students' ability to listen and follow directions by using the Listening Quiz sheet. Use it over and over simply by filling in numbers, letters, symbols, shapes, punctuation marks, or any other indicators that make sense for your purpose, and then creating appropriate directions.

Numbers allow you to create the simplest directions. For example, number each square and give directions like the following:

✸ Place your initials in square #1.

✸ Draw a division symbol in square #5.

✸ Make a happy face in square #12.

You can give more complicated directions if you fill in the squares with a variety of symbols. For example:

✸ Find the clock face. Place hands on it to indicate one o'clock.

✸ Find the shamrock and shade in two of its leaves.

✸ Find the letter C and make in into the letter O.

(See the sample quiz and blank form provided on pages 100–101.)

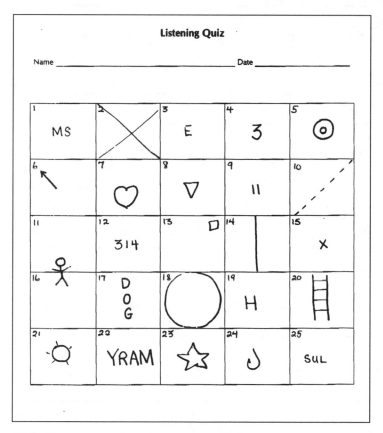

(Solution to sample quiz on page 101)

Name _____ Date _____

Oral Presentation: Listening Critically

Name of Presenter: _____

Evaluating the Content

✶ What is the purpose of the presentation? (to inform, raise awareness, persuade, entertain, thank, introduce, etc.). How do you know?

_____

_____

_____

✶ What are two main points made in the presentation?

(i)_____

_____

_____

(ii)_____

_____

_____

✶ Give details, evidence, or examples that illustrate one of the points.

(i)_____

_____

_____

(ii)_____

_____

_____

✶ What conclusion, solution, or impression does the speaker end with?

_____

_____

_____

_____

(continued…)

75 Language Arts Assessment Tools • Scholastic Teaching Resources

(continued...)

Oral Presentation: Listening Critically

✴ How does the introduction capture the listener's attention?

_____

_____

_____

✴ How does the speaker use his/her voice and pauses to emphasize and dramatize the message?

_____

_____

_____

✴ How does the speaker involve the audience in the presentation?

_____

_____

_____

✴ How does the speaker create an effective conclusion?

_____

_____

_____

Overall Evaluation

✴ What did you like best about the presentation?

_____

_____

_____

✴ Describe one way the content or delivery could be improved.

_____

_____

_____

Name _____ Date _____

Listening Quiz

75 Language Arts Assessment Tools • Scholastic Teaching Resources

Listening Quiz

Directions

NOTE: You may wish to give very explicit directions, such as those suggested in the parentheses for some of the steps below, so that students whose vocabulary is less sophisticated will not be disadvantaged in showing their ability to focus, listen, and follow directions. For students who do poorly on such an activity, ascertain which part of the process is causing the problem: Is it hearing, attention, vocabulary, or uncertainty about actually executing the directions? (Though there are only 24 steps, all 25 squares are used, as step 18 fills two squares.)

1. Place initials for your first and last names in square #1

2. Draw a diamond in a corner of square #13

3. Print the first three letters of your last name in square #25

4. Make a dotted diagonal line (from corner to corner) in square #10

5. Print a 3-digit number in square #12

6. Print the word DOG vertically (from top to bottom) in square #17

7. Draw a sun in square #21

8. Print the fifth letter of the alphabet in square #3

9. Draw an upside-down triangle in square #8

10. Print the number to show your age in square #9

11. Put an x in the middle of Square #15

12. Draw a ladder going vertically (straight up) in the middle of square #20

13. Make a capital letter H in square #19

14. Draw a fish hook in square #24

15. Make an X that connects the corners of square #2

16. Draw an arrow in square #6 that points to the number 6

17. Print a single digit number in square #4

18. Draw a stick man with his head and arms in square #11 and his legs in square #16

19. Draw a circle to fill square #18

20. Draw a star in square #23

21. Draw a straight vertical line that divides square #14 in half (Note: do not explain "vertical" here, so that you can assess knowledge of that vocabulary.)

22. Draw a donut in square #5

23. Draw a heart in square #7

24. Print your first name backwards (with the letters in reverse order) in square #22

TOOLS & INSTRUCTIONS: Speaking

Speaking Checklist:
Student Self-Report

The Speaking Checklist can be used at the beginning of the year as a way of collecting information about student preferences and comfort levels. Use it one or more times later in the year to document changes in attitudes or behaviors. This information can assist you in using the evaluation rubrics for speaking.

Responding to a Presentation

Give students this form prior to hearing the speech of a guest or a classmate. Discuss the aspects referred to here and prepare students to listen for and focus on these points. Their responses will tell you about some of their critical thinking abilities as well as communication skills. This activity will assist them in preparing and assessing their own oral presentations.

Rating an Oral Presentation

Discuss the ratings given by students as compared to your own ratings and give reasons for your evaluation. Also talk about what would have increased the rating in a given area.

Once students are versed in the standards for evaluating a presentation (Responding to a Presentation provides good practice), they can begin using the Rating an Oral Presentation tool. This can be used throughout the year.

Rating Storytelling

By assessing the work of their peers, students become more aware of their own mastery of a skill. Ask particular students to use the Rating Storytelling tool to assess a classmate's storytelling ability, and use their responses to assess their understanding of the criteria of good storytelling. You might have them add or replace criteria on the rating sheet to demonstrate more sophisticated understanding.

Speaking Checklist
Student Self-Report

	Usually	Often	Sometimes	Seldom
I like to share my thoughts with ✷ a partner ✷ a small group ✷ the whole class				
I think about what I am going to say before I speak.				
I like to talk something through before I write about it.				
I ask questions and join in class discussions.				
I tend to interrupt others.				
I am brief and to the point when I speak.				
I tend to repeat myself.				
I like to read aloud.				
I like to take part in skits or plays.				
I like to try character voices and accents				
I like to learn words in other languages.				
I like to use new words I have learned.				

✷ What I would like to do better: _____

_____

✷ How I could begin to do this better: _____

_____

✷ Teacher comments _____

_____

_____

Responding to a Presentation
Speaker/Video

Name of Speaker _____ Date _____

Name of Evaluator _____ Activity _____

The process of analyzing speeches, whether those of others or our own, develops in us a heightened awareness of all that goes into a good speech and how we can improve our presentations. Listen for the organization of content and the criteria for delivery of a presentation by referring to the following questions.

CONTENT

1. What does the presentation attempt to accomplish in terms of an issue or cause? (convince, persuade, raise awareness about…)

   _____

   _____

   _____

   _____

2. What are the main points made by the speaker/video about the problem associated with that issue?

   _____

   _____

   _____

   _____

3. What details or evidence is presented to illustrate these main points?

   _____

   _____

   _____

   _____

4. What solutions are suggested by the speaker/video?

   _____

   _____

   _____

   _____

(continued…)

(continued...)

DELIVERY

5. How does the introduction capture the listener's attention?

_____

_____

_____

_____

6. How does the speaker use voice changes (volume, pitch) and pause to emphasize and dramatize the message?

_____

_____

_____

_____

7. How does the speaker involve the audience in the presentation?

_____

_____

_____

_____

8. How does the speaker/video create an effective conclusion?

_____

_____

_____

_____

9. What did you like best about the presentation?

_____

_____

_____

_____

10. How could the presentation be improved?

_____

_____

_____

Rating an Oral Presentation

Name of Presenter _____ Date _____

Name of Evaluator _____

Rate your classmate's presentation using the criteria below:

4 = strongly agree   3 = agree   2 = disagree   1 = strongly disagree

CONTENT

✸ The purpose of the presentation was clear.   _____

✸ The main points could be followed.   _____

✸ Adequate details supported the main points.   _____

✸ A main impression, conclusion, or solution was suggested.   _____

✸ The speech had unique and original ideas.   _____

DELIVERY

✸ The introduction captured the listener's interest.   _____

✸ The speaker spoke clearly and with a good pace.   _____

✸ The speaker used voice inflection, volume, and pauses to
   emphasize and dramatize the message.   _____

✸ The speaker involved the audience in the presentation.   _____

✸ The speaker created an effective conclusion.   _____

TOTAL SCORE _____

Rating Storytelling

Rate your classmate as a storyteller using the following scale:

4 = strongly agree   3 = agree   2 = disagree   1 = strongly disagree

_____
(name of storyteller)

✳ Related the events in sequence so the story was easy to follow   _____

✳ Used clear, simple sentences   _____

✳ Spoke without stumbling or repeating   _____

✳ Spoke clearly so every word could be understood   _____

✳ Spoke loudly enough that everyone could hear   _____

✳ Spoke with expression using pitch, volume, and tone changes   _____

✳ Used pauses to heighten interest and suspense   _____

✳ Used facial expression to emphasize and dramatize   _____

✳ Used gestures and body language to enhance the story   _____

✳ _____   _____

✳ _____   _____

✳ _____   _____

✳ _____   _____

✳ _____   _____

✳ _____   _____

✳ _____   _____

TOTAL SCORE _____

Assessment and Evaluation of Representing and Viewing

Some curriculum documents refer to representing as a language arts area that includes processes and products that are visual arts, technological media, and other forms of projects that students create to express and share their knowledge. This section of assessment instruments provides checklists and rating criteria for processes and products that do not fit the traditional categories of language arts, or ones that combine several areas.

Some of these activities and products—such as timelines, posters, games, brochures, and surveys—also fall into the social studies area. I have chosen to include the research assessments in this section since they also tend to involve reading, writing, computer skills, and presentation in some form. As with other areas of assessment, it is important for students to participate in, or at least have advance knowledge of, the criteria for assessment.

Again, in this section, you will find instruments that deal with attitudes (Art Reflections, page 131) and with behaviors (Visual Reflections, page 130). There are also instruments that assess students' critical thinking abilities with regard to understanding visual representations, such as Non-Print Information (page 126).

TOOLS & INSTRUCTIONS: Representing

Evaluating a Project

This generic form can be enhanced and reproduced for use with any project or representation. It can also be used as a student checklist for revision purposes.

Rating a Timeline

A rating scale is an effective tool for students' self-evaluation. Invite students to come up with their own rating descriptors—words they can use to describe four levels of achievement in evaluating their work, with four being the highest. Their descriptors may not match yours. Encourage them to use theirs! For example:

4 = Awesome! (excellent)

3 = Pretty decent (good)

2 = OK (satisfactory)

1 = So-so (needs work)

Ask students to discuss what is involved in making a timeline. What steps are required? Ask them to brainstorm, in groups or with partners, some specific things they will need to do to complete each step and create an "excellent" project. Finally, work with them to create a checklist to use for evaluating the effort they put into their project.

Once they understand the process, invite students to evaluate their project work using their brainstormed criteria. (The sheets can be a model for the group's own rating scale, used as is or modified.) To make the students' self-evaluation more realistic, suggest that they talk over their product and presentation with a peer before evaluating them.

You can assess the timelines as well. This step is optional, but very beneficial. If student marks differ from yours, discuss how and why they differ.

Assessing a Timeline
Process and Product

Have students use this form as a checklist to review the work they do on their timelines. If students go through a form like this before they begin the task, they will have a heightened awareness of what the task involves and how they will be evaluated.

Name _____ Date _____

Evaluating a Project
Self-Evaluation

Project _____ Class _____

Modify this form to fit any representation.

4 = excellent **3 = very good** **2 = satisfactory** **1 = needs work**

CONTENT

✳ Effectiveness in accomplishing purpose (did what it was supposed to)

✳ Amount of quality of ideas (enough ideas, good ideas)

✳ Supporting detail (examples, evidence, or description)

Rating 4 3 2 1

STRUCTURE

✳ Logical organization (sequence, order of ideas)

✳ Coherence (hangs together as a whole)

✳ Appropriate and correct format (as a letter, report, survey, etc.)

Rating 4 3 2 1

MECHANICS AND CONVENTIONS

✳ Spelling

✳ Punctuation

✳ Capitalization

✳ Grammar

Rating 4 3 2 1

PRESENTATION

✳ Overall neatness

✳ Special features (charts, drawings, graphs, title page)

Rating 4 3 2 1

MY OVERALL RATING _____

Student Remarks:
What I liked best…How could I do a better job of next time…Whatever!

_____

_____

_____

Rating a Timeline
Teacher-Assessment/Self-Assessment

Activity _____

4 = excellent   3 = very good   2 = satisfactory   1 = needs work

	Student Mark	Teacher Mark
THE STUDENT WORK SHOWS:		
✴ All the possible inclusions		
✴ Information recorded clearly and accurately		
✴ Information selected from more than one source		
✴ Events ordered correctly by dates		
✴ The effects of revision and more than one draft		
✴ Inclusion of artwork (symbols, drawings, clipart)		
✴ An interesting layout for text and visuals		
✴ A final copy that is neat and attractive		
✴ Correct spelling and punctuation		

Student Mark   Teacher Mark

_____   _____

Assessing a Timeline
Process and Product

Use this assessment as a check of your own timeline or a peer's work. Make changes as necessary before handing it in for marking.

How well you prepared:

✹ How much thinking did you do to come up with something interesting?

✹ Did you make notes when you brainstormed ideas for your topic?

✹ If you made a personal timeline, did you talk to your family, look through albums, etc.?

✹ If you chose a topic or period, did you check it out in the library or on the Internet?

Changes to be made: _____

_____

_____

_____

_____

How well you drafted the events:

✹ How thoroughly did you brainstorm ideas for your timeline?

✹ Did you collect as much information as possible to begin with?

✹ If you did research, did you record the information you found clearly and accurately?

✹ If you did a personal timeline, did you choose information from different times in your life?

✹ Did you select information that would show different aspects of your life, such as sports, health, family moves, important friends, etc.?

✹ Did you check to see that the events were ordered correctly by date?

Changes to be made: _____

_____

_____

_____

_____

(continued...)

(continued...)

Assessing a Timeline

How well you revised and edited:

✹ Did you have someone respond to your draft before you made the final copy?

✹ Did you make changes to improve your work?

✹ Did you make sure that spelling and punctuation were correct?

✹ Did you include artwork and photos?

✹ Did you create an interesting layout for your text and visuals?

✹ Did you make the final copy as neat and attractive as possible?

Changes to be made: _____

_____

_____

_____

_____

_____

Rating a Brochure

Presenting a sample (or several samples) of brochures done by former students together with the Rating a Brochure form allows you to demonstrate the expectations for this product. Students may also use this tool for self- and peer-evaluation.

Computer Project

While this tool is designed for self-assessment, you may prefer that students do the Computer Project assessment in conference rather than independently in writing. Debriefing in pairs or small groups may encourage more discussion and sharing of possibilities than written response does.

Use of Research Sources

This form helps students to reflect on the process of their research, and especially upon the extent of their search for information.

Research: Knowledge of the Process

Asking students to respond to some or all of the questions on this sheet will provide evidence of their knowledge of the research process and their use of appropriate research skills.

Assessing Research Process
Teacher Notes

Use the Assessing Research Process tool in a conference setting to help you assess student performance in research projects.

Name _Bradley_   Date _2/13_

Assessing Research Process
Teacher Notes

Project Title: _Hear Ye, Hear Ye_

Resources Considered	Resources Used
Internet	
Library Resources	
Science text	Primary Science Text: The World of the Senses

✱ Help requested: _none_

✱ How well the information was used: _Brad didn't get started until the last class period. He had grand ideas about what he would do, but in the end, used only the primary text._

✱ New skills learned or practiced: _I don't think Brad learned much from this project – except perhaps that he needs to ask for help and get started much sooner._

✱ What the student found most difficult: _Brad couldn't come up with a realistic/manageable way to demonstrate his concept (to show 3rd graders how sound travels). He was disorganized and unprepared because he got such a late start. Next time Brad says he'll start sooner and come up with an outline._

120

75 Language Arts Assessment Tools • Scholastic Teaching Resources

Name _____ Date _____

Rating a Brochure

Activity _____ Class _____

Assign marks for each point using the following rating scale:

4 = excellent   **3 = very good**   **2 = satisfactory**   **1 = needs work**

✹ The student(s) presented the key information needed in the brochure.	4	3	2	1
✹ The student(s) used spaces provided effectively.	4	3	2	1
✹ The student(s) provided sufficient detail to support the necessary information.	4	3	2	1
✹ The student(s) balanced visuals with the print.	4	3	2	1
✹ The brochure was eye-catching and colorful.	4	3	2	1
✹ The visuals were realistic and easy to understand.	4	3	2	1
✹ The information and visuals presented on the brochure were original.	4	3	2	1
✹ The overall presentation of the brochure was appealing and effective.	4	3	2	1

TOTAL SCORE _____

75 Language Arts Assessment Tools • Scholastic Teaching Resources

Name _____ Date _____

Computer Project
Self-Assessment

Project _____ Class _____

✶ Briefly describe your project: _____

_____

_____

✶ What audience is this project intended for? What was the response of that audience to your project?

_____

_____

✶ What main purpose did it have?

_____

_____

✶ Was that purpose achieved? Explain: _____

_____

✶ What part of the project were you most satisfied with? Why?

_____

_____

✶ What gave you the most challenge or difficulty? Why?

_____

_____

✶ What new skill or knowledge did you gain doing this project?

_____

_____

✶ What would you do differently another time?

_____

_____

Name _____ Date _____

Use of Research Sources

Project Title/Description _____

Types of Resources		Details	Checked	Used
Print:	book			
	magazine			
	newspaper			
	other			
Media:	documentary			
	TV			
	video			
	other			
Computer:	CD-Rom			
	Internet			
	other			
People:	individuals			
	survey			
	organizations			

✴ New skills I learned or practiced: _____

_____

_____

✴ What I enjoyed most about doing this research: _____

_____

_____

(Use the back of the sheet if you wish.)

75 Language Arts Assessment Tools • Scholastic Teaching Resources

Research: Knowledge of the Process

Imagine that you are doing a research project about weather. Answer these questions to show what you know about researching a topic.

✷ What is the very first thing that must be clear in your mind before you begin the project?

_____

_____

_____

✷ Name three possible sources of information you can think of for this topic. Be specific.

a) _____

b) _____

c) _____

✷ How could you use those sources to gather information? _____

_____

_____

✷ Describe three things you could do so you won't have to read or view the whole resource to see if it has any information you can use.

a) _____

b) _____

c) _____

✷ Describe two important parts you would include in your final report.

a) _____

_____

b) _____

_____

✷ Why is it important to know the purpose and audience for your research before you start?

_____

_____

_____

Name _____ Date _____

Assessing Research Process
Teacher Notes

Project Title: _____

Resources Considered	Resources Used

★ Help requested: _____

_____

_____

_____

★ How well the information was used: _____

_____

_____

_____

★ New skills learned or practiced: _____

_____

_____

_____

★ What the student found most difficult: _____

_____

_____

_____

75 Language Arts Assessment Tools • Scholastic Teaching Resources

TOOLS & INSTRUCTIONS: Viewing

Visual Arts Project
Peer Evaluation

This form will assist students in evaluating peer presentations. It is helpful at times to show students what marks you would assign for each category, after they have already scored a presentation themselves. This way, student evaluations need not be made known to presenters, while students still gain critical skills by comparing their evaluations to yours. Rather than emphasizing the presenter, the marks can be discussed in the context of the evaluator's thinking.

Reading Pictures

Use the Reading Pictures tool to document students' response to and analysis of the visuals in a magazine or book. Have individuals respond to any visuals you or they wish to use—whatever meets your assessment needs. This is very useful with social studies material, newspaper and magazine visuals, as well as with illustrations in literature.

You can further assess the level of sophistication, prior knowledge, critical thinking skills, and imagination that students bring to bear on non-print text by having them respond to one or more pictures either in conference with you or independently in writing.

Assessing a Visual Presentation
Self-Portrait

After you assess students' visual self-portraits, have them assess their own as well, using selected questions from the Assessing a Visual Presentation sheet. Be sure to make the students aware of how and why your assessments differ from theirs, if they do.

Seeing Beyond Print

Have students look at the purposes behind the non-print elements in non-fiction books. Use the Seeing Beyond Print sheet as review from time to time, if necessary.

Non-Print Information

Follow up on a Seeing Beyond Print review by asking students to study and comment on one or more of the book's visuals (depending on your specific assessment needs), using the Non-Print Information sheet. Have them describe each visual they select, state what purpose it serves, and comment on how effective it is.

Name _____ Date _____

Visual Arts Project
Peer Evaluation

Presenter's Name _____ Date _____

Evaluator's Name _____ Activity _____

Give the presenter a mark of 1, 2, or 3 (3 being the highest).

✵ The message or information was presented clearly.   _____

✵ It was presented in an interesting way.   _____

✵ The purpose of the presentation was evident.   _____

✵ The presentation showed that the presenter knew how to use this medium or form (art, photos, movie, etc.) and the necessary materials or equipment.   _____

✵ The presentation seemed fluent and polished.   _____

✵ The title was a good one.   _____

TOTAL SCORE   _____

✵ The thing I liked best about the presentation was…

_____

_____

_____

_____

✵ One suggestion I would make for next time is…

_____

_____

_____

_____

75 Language Arts Assessment Tools • Scholastic Teaching Resources

Reading Pictures

✷ Page _____ Description of picture: _____

_____

_____

What I feel when I see this picture, and why: _____

_____

_____

What I know or guess about its subject: _____

_____

_____

What questions come to my mind: _____

_____

_____

✷ Page _____ Description of picture: _____

_____

_____

What I feel when I see this picture, and why: _____

_____

_____

What I know or guess about its subject: _____

_____

_____

What questions come to my mind: _____

_____

_____

Assessing a Visual Presentation
Self-Portrait

Use the following questions to look critically at the sketch, painting, or collage you created as a self-portrait.

✯ What is there in this visual that links it unmistakably to me? _____

_____

_____

_____

✯ What important aspects of my identity have I represented? _____

_____

_____

_____

✯ How have I used space, form, or color to say something about myself?_____

_____

_____

_____

✯ What did I learn about myself while creating this visual? _____

_____

_____

_____

✯ What do I wish I could have done better in creating this self-portrait? _____

_____

_____

_____

75 Language Arts Assessment Tools • Scholastic Teaching Resources

Seeing Beyond Print

The pictures in a magazine or book give you different kinds of information than print does. In non-fiction materials you can find information in drawings, paintings, photographs, diagrams, cartoons, graphs, charts, maps, and forms. Color, shading, information set off in boxes, captions, even blank spaces—all of these elements of design have a purpose. Thinking about why these elements are used in a piece of non-fiction will help you to understand the information that is being presented.

Some of the purposes for non-print information are:

✺ to describe or explain

✺ to instruct in a procedure

✺ to diagram and label parts

✺ to compare

✺ to capture the viewer's attention

✺ to present complex information in a limited space

✺ to show the relationship between two or more parts

✺ to show how several parts are interrelated in the "big picture"

✺ to capture the personal or human aspect (e.g., feelings)

✺ to help the viewer analyze data

Select specific elements used in the book you are reading and comment on them using the Non-Print Information sheet (page 126), as in this sample.

Name _____   Date _____

Non-Print Information

Title of book/article __Knights in Rusty Armour__   Page # ___62-63___

✺ Description of picture
   __Drawings of medieval weapons__
   _____

✺ Purpose of picture
   __To name these weapons and show what they looked like__
   _____

✺ Techniques and effectiveness
   __Putting several weapons side by side shows how they compare in size—__
   __putting them around the edge of the text adds information not in__
   __the text__
   _____

Non-Print Information

Title of book/article _____ Page #_____

★ Description of picture:

_____

_____

★ Purpose of picture:

_____

_____

★ Techniques and effectiveness:

_____

_____

_____

_____

Title of book/article _____ Page #_____

★ Description of picture:

_____

_____

★ Purpose of picture:

_____

_____

★ Techniques and effectiveness:

_____

_____

_____

_____

TOOLS & INSTRUCTIONS: Visual Behaviors and Reflections

Viewing Behaviors

It is easy to overlook what can be learned about comprehension from observing viewing behaviors. The Viewing Behaviors checklist gives you a tool for documenting those behaviors. This can be reproduced and used throughout the year to record developments and changes as the year progresses.

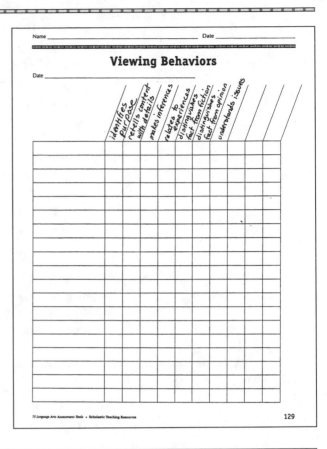

Visual Reflections
Self-Report

The Visual Reflections checklist provides you with information about your students' skills and behaviors with respect to visual representation, and about their perception of themselves as artists. Have them report on *how frequently*, *how comfortably*, and *how well* they do the activities listed, and any others you might want to assess. Before they use the sheet, run through the following "level" descriptors with them to give them an idea how to answer:

how frequently
   4 = whenever I can
   3 = often
   2 = sometimes
   1 = not unless I have to

how comfortably
   4 = very comfortably
   3 = fairly comfortably
   2 = with some effort
   1 = with a lot of effort or help

how well
   4 = I'm really good at it
   3 = I'm pretty good at it
   2 = I think I do OK but I'm not sure
   1 = I don't think I'm very good at it

In the Student Comments section of this tool, let students know that they can comment on whether or not they enjoy drawing and why. They might also note what sorts of visual representations they prefer making, and what presentations they have viewed or created that have featured the use of illustrations.

Art Reflections

Having students use the Art Reflections tool to describe and reflect on the process and product of their own art activity will make them more aware of the criteria you use in judging their work.

Judging My Poster

Ask students to use the Judging My Poster sheet to help them assess their posters. Their posters and their responses will help you decide which students need more opportunities to practice visual representation.

Name _____ Date _____

Viewing Behaviors

Date _____

Name _____ Date _____

Visual Reflections
Self Report

For each of the statements below, rate yourself from 1-4 (with 4 being the highest) for how frequently, how comfortably, and how well you do the specified activity. (A *4* in the "frequently" column would indicate very frequently and a *1* would mean "infrequently." Similarly, a *4* for comfort would be "very comfortably" but a *1* would be "not comfortably at all."

	Frequently	Comfortably	Well
✯ I make sketches to help get ideas for my writing and artwork.			
✯ I sketch ideas, notes, and/or vocabulary concepts.			
✯ I enjoy making pictures for stories, title pages, and posters.			
✯ I like doing diagrams.			
✯ I sometimes share information using block pictures, like a comic strip.			
✯ I use visual organizers like boxes, arrows and circles to organize my ideas and to display information.			
SUBTOTALS:			

TOTAL SCORE: _____

Comments:

_____

_____

_____

_____

_____

_____

75 Language Arts Assessment Tools • Scholastic Teaching Resources

Art Reflections

Look carefully at a painting, sketch, poster, or collage you have created. Complete the following statements to reflect on your work.

✸ I would describe my artwork as:

_____

_____

_____

✸ The message or impression I want to give to the people viewing it is:

_____

_____

_____

✸ What I enjoyed most about creating it is:

_____

_____

_____

✸ Next time I create a piece of art I'm going to try:

_____

_____

_____

✸ Creating this art helped me to learn:

_____

_____

_____

✸ Teacher comments

_____

_____

_____

Judging My Poster

Use the following questions to look carefully at your sketch, painting, or collage and judge its effectiveness as a poster.

✦ Is the message I wanted to give viewers clear on my poster? (Explain.)

_____

_____

_____

_____

_____

✦ What is eye-catching or effective about the way I have used space, form, or color to make people notice my poster?

_____

_____

_____

✦ How have I shown viewers the importance of this concept?

_____

_____

_____

✦ What have I learned by working on this poster?

_____

_____

_____

✦ Some ideas I learned from my classmates' posters:

_____

_____

_____

TOOLS & INSTRUCTIONS: Representation and the Media

Show by Drawing

Assess your students' abilities to use drawings to summarize the events and show the structure of a story by using the Show by Drawing tool. If necessary, review with students how to represent the main structure of a story in sequenced picture blocks. Then read a story from a magazine (or another source) while they take notes to record names, key words, etc. Finally, ask students to draw what they think represents the main structure of the story, using no less than three sequenced pictures and no more than five. Have them add a one-sentence caption to each picture if they wish. Evaluate their drawings based on the way they include:

- � The main characters
- � The central conflict
- � A beginning, middle, and end
- � Appropriate details
- � Sensible captions

This activity gives you a good idea of how well students grasp main ideas (events) that create the basic plot structure.

Media Watch— What I See Media Watch— What I Think

Assessing how your students view and evaluate media messages will help you use the viewing rubric.

Because television, video, and film are so prominent in our culture today, students need to develop the ability to view these media in an informed and critical manner. As they become increasingly sophisticated in their understanding of media, students begin to respond on an aesthetic level; to understand that messages are constructed for particular purposes; and to question the underlying commercial, social, and political implications in the popular media.

Have students watch a selected television commercial, using the Media Watch—What I See sheet to make notes on it as they watch. Then have them use the Media Watch—What I Think sheet to record their evaluations of it. When they have finished, you can assess their responses. As students gain more critical experience, this tool might be adjusted to use in an analysis of infomercials, television news reports/shows, political speeches, etc.

Show by Drawing

Title	1
2	**3**
4	**5**

75 Language Arts Assessment Tools • Scholastic Teaching Resources

Media Watch—What I See

Use this page to make notes on a television commercial you watch.

✸ Product: _____

✸ Advertiser: _____

✸ Length of commercial: _____

✸ How many times does the commercial show the product? _____

✸ How many times does the advertiser's name appear in the commercial? _____

✸ Does the commercial move slowly or quickly? _____

✸ Is there music? If so, describe the music and give your opinion of it: _____

_____

_____

_____

✸ The commercial uses: people   animals   cartoons   other

✸ This is what happens: _____

_____

_____

_____

✸ The message is presented by: an on-screen announcer   a voice-over   other

✸ (Explain "other.") _____

✸ This is how the message is presented: _____

_____

_____

_____

_____

_____

Name ______________________ Date ______________

Media Watch—What I Think

Think about the notes you took using the Media Watch—What I See sheet. Now evaluate the commercial by giving your opinions.

- What is the main message of the commercial?

- What do you think of the main message?

- What do you think about the commercial as a whole? Why?

- Would you buy the product? Why?

- Teacher comments

Group Work and Participation

In this section, you will find instruments that deal with assessment of the interpersonal and management skills that allow students to work effectively, both individually and in groups. Encourage students to be reflective about how the group has worked as a unit, as well as how they themselves have contributed to the group effort. Raising the level of awareness of these skills will enhance the development of collaborative skills. Groups and individuals can use the feedback from these evaluations to set measurable goals and targets for improvement. You can use the occasion of group work to observe student skills in other areas as well, including speaking, listening, and critical thinking.

TOOLS & INSTRUCTIONS: Group Behaviors

Participation Behaviors

Use the Participation Behaviors checklist to document collaborative behaviors you observe informally during group work times. You may decide to monitor these behaviors on a regular basis. Your observations will help inform your judgment about individual students as readers, viewers, speakers, and listeners.

You can certainly use the information documented here together with the students' own Participation Checklist and your Rating Group Work sheet to help you get a more complete assessment of collaboration skills.

Participation Behaviors

Date _____

listens attentively / *encourages others* / *volunteers answers* / *invites feedback* / *makes personal notes* / *volunteers to record* / *shares ideas and opinions* / *takes on a specific task*

75 Language Arts Assessment Tools • Scholastic Teaching Resources

139

Participation Checklist

The Participation Checklist encourages students to reflect on their habits and behaviors as members of a learning community. It provides an occasion for discussion of these aspects of learning, either in individual conferences or as a class. It also offers an opportunity for students to evaluate and set goals for themselves.

Use the comment space to suggest strategies, affirm positive behaviors, or ask a question to help the student focus on an area in which he or she might grow.

Rating Group Work
Self/Group/Teacher Evaluation

Use this tool to show students some criteria for judging how effectively we can collaborate. Share these criteria with students before they begin to remind them that you will be monitoring the group to see how well they are meeting these criteria from day to day as they work on the project. Have the criteria posted to heighten their awareness of the goals for working together.

Assessment of Collaborative Skills
Self-Evaluation and Teacher/Peer Evaluation

These two instruments encourage students to become more aware of how they interact and contribute in team projects.

Once completed, these forms are highly effective tools and terrific discussion resources for individual student-teacher conferences. The additional lines may be used for specific collaboration skills you wish to assess, or for related comments.

Participation Behaviors

Date _____

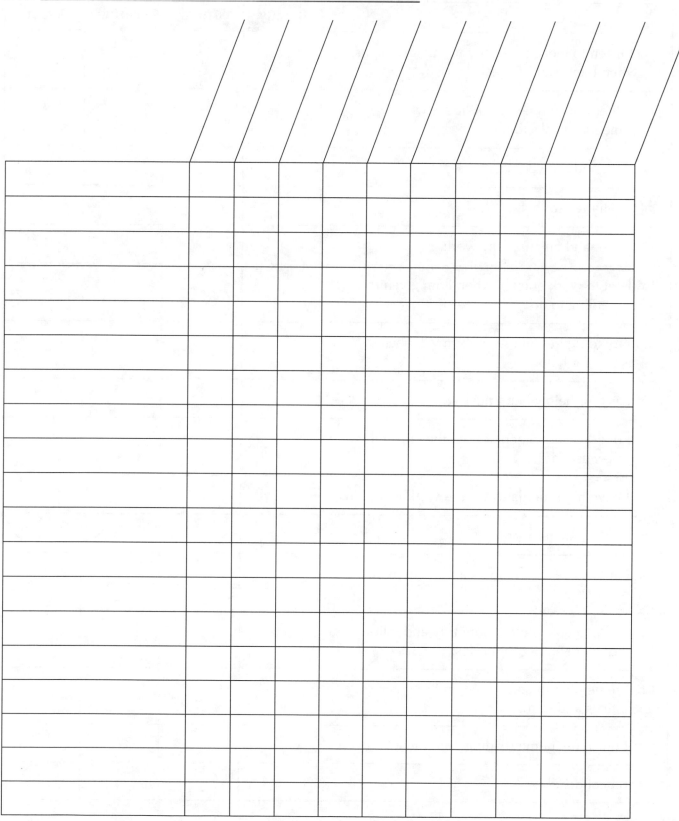

Participation Checklist

	Usually	Often	Sometimes	Seldom
☆ I listen to the teacher and to other students when they read or speak.				
☆ I offer my comments and ideas when someone speaks to me.				
☆ I ask and answer questions.				
☆ I volunteer to help.				
☆ I plan and organize my work.				
☆ I get to work quickly when I am given something to do.				
☆ I try to figure things out for myself before asking for help.				
☆ I ask for help when I need it.				
☆ I offer to help others if I see they need it, or if they ask for it.				
☆ I have high standards for the work I hand in.				
☆ I do my share of group work.				
☆ I am courteous to others and include them in activities.				
☆ I help keep my classroom tidy and follow classroom and school rules.				
☆ I remember to take home and return notices and forms.				
☆ I finish my home reading and homework.				
☆ I meet deadlines.				

(continued...)

75 Language Arts Assessment Tools • Scholastic Teaching Resources

Name _____ Date _____

(continued...)

Participation Checklist

✸ What I would like to do better:

_____

_____

_____

_____

_____

_____

_____

✸ How I can do this better:

_____

_____

_____

_____

_____

_____

_____

✸ Teacher comments

_____

_____

_____

_____

_____

_____

_____

Rating Group Work
Self/Group/Teacher Evaluation

Activity _____   Class _____

4	3	2	1
Most of the time **Most of the members** **Highly evident** **Excellent**			**Seldom** **Only 1 or 2 members** **Hardly evident** **Weak**

	4	3	2	1
✶ During brainstorming, all students participated by listening, contributing, encouraging.	4	3	2	1
✶ The group was careful to divide up the work fairly and evenly.	4	3	2	1
✶ The members completed their work within the time they set for themselves as a group.	4	3	2	1
✶ The members discussed and helped one another with problems and challenges.	4	3	2	1
✶ The group shared decision-making about the important parts of the work	4	3	2	1
✶ The group worked in an orderly and purposeful way.	4	3	2	1

TOTAL _____

Assessment of Collaborative Skills
Self-Evaluation

Rate yourself as a group participant according to your performance in this unit. Use the following indicators:

VG = Very Good   I = Improved   SNW = Still Needs Work

_____ I come prepared for the group activity.

_____ I listen carefully and respectfully.

_____ I respond clearly and honestly.

_____ I attempt answers.

_____ I make suggestions.

_____ I encourage or invite others to contribute.

_____ I make sure I know what the task is.

_____ I can be depended on to record accurately for the group.

_____ I can participate without bothering others.

_____ I get down to the task quickly.

_____ I give help to others when asked.

_____ I complete what is expected or assigned.

_____   _____

_____   _____

_____   _____

_____   _____

_____   _____

Assessment of Collaborative Skills
Teacher/Peer Evaluation

Rate the following team skills as:

VG = Very Good   **I = Improved**   **SNW = Still Needs Work**

_____ Comes prepared for the group activity.

_____ Listens carefully and respectfully.

_____ Responds clearly and honestly.

_____ Attempts answers.

_____ Makes suggestions.

_____ Encourages or invites others to contribute.

_____ Can be depended on to record accurately for the group.

_____ Knows what the task is, or asks for clarification.

_____ Participates without bothering others.

_____ Gets down to the task quickly.

_____ Gives help to others when asked.

_____ Responsibly completes what is expected or assigned.

_____ _____

_____ _____

_____ _____

_____ _____

_____ _____

_____ _____

Rubrics

Rubrics can be created for at least two fundamentally different purposes:

1. To provide a general evaluation of student skills as seen over time, or across a spectrum of interwoven abilities that comprise a broader ability concept, such as literacy or critical thinking

2. To provide an evaluation based on a specific task or assignment

General evaluation rubrics provide a global perspective by describing student develop–ment in a particular area, such as research skills or applying concepts. In a sense, the assessment instruments presented here can, together with those created by you, contribute to an eventual "summing up"—an evaluation of a student's performance against expectations or criteria set by curriculum. Examples of general rubrics for each of the language arts strands (reading, writing, listening, speaking, viewing, and representing) are provided here to assist you in achieving general descriptions of a student's abilities.

Four-level rubrics are provided since levels of literacy have a critical bearing on the ability to communicate information and ideas. Do not hesitate to adapt these by adding or modifying descriptors to more accurately reflect aspects of your program's focus. This modification will be particularly important where these rubrics are used directly in reporting to parents.

Task-specific rubrics outline a task to be performed and describe several levels of response to the task. These rubrics refer to specific behaviors or aspects of performance on a graduated scale, from low-level, unsophisticated responses to highly competent and sophisticated responses.

Although most of the rubrics presented in this section are broad-based and general in scope, both task-specific and general rubrics are provided. Some specific tasks are also presented together with a rubric to give you examples of the kinds of assessments and measurements the rubrics can help you make. Using these and other rubrics as models, you may also wish to create your own rubrics for particular tasks or assignments. A tip sheet for creating such rubrics is provided (see Creating a Rubric, page 157), as well as an example of a task-specific rubric (see Biographical Profile, page 79).

Another valuable undertaking is to show students how rubrics are created and used. This activity will make students more aware of the specific aspects of performance you are looking for and using in the evaluation. When students assist in creating the rubric, they find it easier to focus on and produce the desired outcome. (See Student-Created Rubrics on page 156; for an example of a teacher-created rubric, see Evaluating a Summary on pages 67–68.)

To use the rubrics effectively, gather information from a variety of sources. The tools in this book will assist you in collecting information about learners' knowledge, skills, and attitudes. **The more contexts and sources used to observe and document a performance, the sharper and truer will be the picture of that student's development as an intelligent, competent, and literate individual.**

Reading

Collect appropriate data for use with the reading using the tools in the Assessment &
Evaluation of Reading section, as well as from formal evaluations (reading tests) and from
observed daily reading behaviors.

The student...

Highest Level			Lowest Level
silent-reads fluently the grade-level text and reference material	reads grade-level text and reference material with understanding and efficiency	finds it difficult to read independently grade-level text and reference material	guesses at many words and (without assistance) extracts little meaning from the text or reference material at grade level
is able to retell accurately the main points, supply most of the supporting detail, make and understand inferences, make sensible predictions and hypotheses	is able to retell, with a fair degree of accuracy, the main points and the supporting detail, make/understand most inferences, make sensible predictions	is able to retell some main points and supply some supporting detail, understands few inferences, is able to make only few or weak predictions	retells few of the ideas and details—without sequence/organization and without distinction between main idea and supporting detail, is unable to make inferences or sensible predictions
confidently identifies distinctions between fact, fiction, and opinion	identifies distinctions between fact, fiction, and opinion	has real difficulty identifying distinctions between fact and opinion	is unable to identify distinctions between fact and opinion
reads aloud fluently and expressively, pronouncing almost all words correctly	reads aloud with fluency and some expression, pronouncing most words correctly	is able to read the text at a slow rate with sensible phrasing and inflection; some words are mispronounced or require more than one attempt to correct	reads haltingly, without phrasing or appropriate response to punctuation; mispronounces words, is often unable to self-correct
is able independently to identify and locate appropriate reference sources, uses skimming and scanning to efficiently extract information	is able, in most cases, to locate reference sources, and make use of some scanning techniques to extract information	is able, with assistance, to locate reference sources, but may require assistance to extract appropriate information; needs prompting to read at different rates for different purposes	is unable to locate reference sources and has difficulty knowing what information to extract; is unable to read at different rates for different purposes
is an avid reader and chooses to read in spare time at school	reads when the opportunity is presented; sometimes reads for recreation	reads only when required to do so, does not read for pleasure	is unable to focus on silent reading, does not choose to read in any circumstance

146

Writing

Collect data for use with these rubrics by using the instruments in the Assessment & Evaluation of Writing section, through written responses on tests and assignments, and especially through work done with students on revisions of their work.

Highest Level			Lowest Level
uses one or more methods (talking/ discussing, brainstorming, webbing, outlining) to generate several good ideas for writing; writes willingly and with confidence	generates good ideas for writing; writes willingly and with confidence	generates adequate material with assistance through peer discussion, teacher-led activities, or the use of visual organizers; writes only for necessary purposes	generates inadequate material even with assistance; dislikes writing and enters the process reluctantly
leads from the topic; sequences; uses transition; organizes in paragraph units; includes relevant, interesting detail/example to develop the main ideas	leads from the topic, presents relevant ideas in coherent paragraphs with some supporting detail/example	stays on topic and presents material to develop the topic, although ideas may be somewhat unoriginal or uninteresting	writes about the subject, but not necessarily the topic; work shows no organizational framework.
composes a variety of formats (letter, report, story, article) for appropriate purposes	writes common formats (letter, report, story, article) for appropriate purposes	writes in various formats, but with direction and example	has little understanding of or skill with the various modes and formats
uses conventions of spelling, punctuation, and grammar with a high degree of accuracy	uses most conventions of punctuation and grammar with accuracy, spells common words correctly, spells some unfamiliar words phonetically or close to correctly	uses common conventions with satisfactory accuracy, but experiences difficulty with specialized punctuation (e.g., quotations, capitals for nouns of address); spells most common words correctly	has difficulty with common conventions of spelling and punctuation, makes many errors, and corrects only as instructed, often without understanding the concept
uses a variety of sentence patterns and sophisti-cated vocabulary; work demonstrates originality of idea or expression	uses language fluently and avoids slang, written expression is clear and has consistent style and voice	uses basic vocabulary properly and avoids (or uses incorrectly) more complex language; sentences tend to follow a repetitious and simple pattern	uses basic vocabulary, slang, clichés, poor grammar, and sloppy diction
work shows polish achieved through inde-pendent revision and editing	work shows development through revision and editing	work is typically edited (with assistance) for spelling and revised only in response to teacher suggestion	is unable to edit or revise except by following directions to make specific changes

The student...

Listening

Collect data for use with the listening rubrics via the tools in the Assessment & Evaluation of Listening and Speaking section, from formal evaluations (listening tests), and from observations of daily listening behaviors.

The student...

Highest Level			Lowest Level
is able through listening to ascertain the purpose behind an oral presentation and the main ideas it contains	is able through listening to ascertain the purpose behind an oral presentation and supply most of the key points	is able to ascertain through listening the general gist of the presentation	tells what the topic of the presentation is, but is unable to identify the purpose or the main idea of the presentation
is able to supply many accurate details from the presentation	is able to supply most of the details from the presentation	is able to supply some details from the presentation	is able to recall some facts or details of the presentation, but cannot retell these accurately or in order
is able to comment on the perspective, form, and style, including aspects of tone, clarity, and sophistication of the speaker	is able to identify the basic emotional stance, interest, or bias of the speaker, but without necessarily providing the rationale for the conclusions reached	is able to supply some pertinent comments or an accurate general impression of the speaker	is unable to comment meaningfully or accurately about the voice behind the presentation as pertains to stance, tone, or style
is able to make notes and formulate questions or criticisms that demonstrate that the material has been analyzed and evaluated	is able to formulate a reasonable response or rebuttal to the presentation	is able to respond personally to the presentation with some relevant comment from experience or knowledge of the topic	has little or no evaluative comments or relevant response to the presentation
is able to follow directions, and does so with accuracy and without requiring repetition of the information	is able to follow directions with little error or difficulty	is able to follow directions, getting most of the instructions right with some repetition of directions	is unable to follow directions easily or demonstrate accurate response; may give up part way through due to an inability to focus or keep pace
follows group discussion with attention and comprehension as evidenced by participation, body posture, and follow-up activities	generally follows group discussion with attention and understanding	sporadically follows group discussion	is seldom focused on group discussion

Sample Tasks for Assessment of Listening Skills

The tasks presented here can be done with groups, the entire class, or individual students.

Note: The way you ask for the information will make a difference in students' responses. You might ask them to answer specific questions or outline a talk by stating its overall purpose or the main points. These different approaches will give you different kinds of information about students' listening skills and about their mental orientation to information. Some will be good at answering specific questions and others will be able to frame the global perspective.

Task 1: Comprehending/Gaining Information
Have students listen to an oral or taped presentation. (This could be a reading that you present from their text or another source, a presentation by a guest speaker, or an excerpt from an audiotape.) Tell students that they will be required to answer questions and/or comment on aspects of the presentation/recording after they have heard it.

If you want to assess their **ability to gain information by any means**, you can encourage students to take notes during the presentation. If you want to assess their **ability to concentrate and hold main points in their heads** without notes, restrict them to listening only. If you want to assess their **ability to comprehend or retell** aspects of the talk, create short answer or open-ended questions asking for the kind of information you are interested in—for example, detail or main ideas.

Important Note: If the students you are assessing are very weak writers, Task 1 should be done either with the help of a "scribe" or "secretary," or simply be done orally one-on-one. Otherwise the writing task will be a barrier to assessing the listening ability.

Task 2: Following Directions
Present students with a listening activity that requires them to follow paper and pencil directions, marking items on the grid, folding paper according to instructions, or using particular colors and symbols on a map. (See Listening Quiz and the accompanying grid in the Assessment and Evaluation of Listening & Speaking section, pages 100–101.)

Task 3: Following Directions
Use a subject textbook for testing students' ability to listen and follow directions. Create a list of instructions that have to do with turning to certain pages and finding particular features. **This could alternately be used as an assessment of scanning or skimming** by having students scan headings and visuals to locate information, key words, or certain features. **Do this often to keep students continually sharpening their listening and concentration skills**.

Repeat Tasks 2 and 3, giving the same directions as on the earlier attempts but reducing the number of times you repeat the directions on subsequent trials, eventually giving the directions only once. Make instructions progressively longer and more complex to see who can "stay with you." Trying different approaches such as these will give students insight into their strengths and weaknesses in listening skills and will focus you on instructional strategies that support students in developing specific listening skills.
Information gathered through documenting student performance on these tasks will be useful in making judgments in conjunction with the rubric for evaluating listening skills.

Speaking

Collect data for use with these rubrics using the tools related to speaking in the Assessment & Evaluation of Listening and Speaking section, and by observing student speech and communication behaviors in both formal and informal situations.

The student...

Highest Level			Lowest Level
speaks comfortably in everyday situations, often initiating conversation, making needs and opinions known, asking for help, responding to the verbal interactions	speaks comfortably among friends, initiating conversation, making needs and opinions known, asking for help, responding to verbal interaction	makes needs and opinions known to friends and other appropriate individuals; responds to speech directed at him/her	may not be comfortable in communicating needs unless asked; asks a peer or family member to speak on his/her behalf
participates actively in group discussions	participates in group discussion	participates in group discussion only to clarify or ask for help	does not speak up in a group, even to ask for assistance or clarification
speaks at a moderate volume and pace, with clear articulation and expression	speaks at a moderate volume and pace, with clear articulation	speaks clearly in a voice which can be heard by those intended	may speak in a voice that is inaudible or muffled; has poor diction or other difficulties that interfere with articulation
speaks confidently and fluently to an audience including members other than peers	speaks comfortably to a small audience of peers or younger students	speaks when necessary to a small audience of peers or younger students	refuses to speak, or speaks with reluctance, in front of any audience
uses sophisticated vocabulary and precise language in clear and organized presentation	uses appropriate language in a sensible, straight-forward delivery	uses some slang and informal usage to deliver a message that can be understood by its intended audience	uses incorrect grammar, imprecise language, and awkward constructions
chooses examples and details to explain or elaborate	presents some detail and examples to explain and illustrate	presents a basic message satisfactorily, but without much or any elaboration	message is disorganized and unclear, frequently requiring repetition to communicate meaning
uses language in original ways (humor, figurative language, interesting style)	has some repertoire of language uses in different contexts	uses plain language in predictable ways	uses extremely plain and informal language; becomes frustrated and may even choose not to communicate at all

75 Language Arts Assessment Tools • Scholastic Teaching Resources

Representing

Collect data for use with the representing rubrics using the tools dealing with representing in the Assessment & Evaluation of Representing and Viewing section, and by using artifacts themselves—demonstrations, charts, artwork, computer projects, multimedia projects, etc. It is important to note that a single task will not give you all of the necessary information.

The student...

Highest Level			Lowest Level
uses a variety of media, such as visual representation (e.g. symbols, pictures), dramatic representation (e.g. role-playing), and computer representation (e.g. charts, graphs, animation) to aid in exploring, clarifying, and understanding information and ideas in print and other media	uses some forms of representation to aid in clarifying and comprehending ideas in print and other media	satisfactorily uses at least one form of representation other than written text to aid in clarifying and comprehending ideas in print and other media	is not aware of or inclined to use strategies for exploring or clarifying information through various non-print representations
has knowledge of a variety of media (forms and modalities) for generating, organizing, assessing, and sharing ideas and information	has knowledge of some forms and modalities for generating, organizing, assessing, and sharing ideas and information	has limited knowledge of more than one method of representation for generating, organizing, assessing, and sharing ideas and information	has little or no knowledge of forms and modalities other than print
has skill in the techniques for representing ideas and information through a variety of media (forms and modalities)	satisfactorily represents ideas and information through more than one modality	represents ideas and information adequately through at least one modality other than print	is unable and/or uninterested in generating, organizing, assessing, and sharing ideas through drawing, visualizing, role-playing, and other representations
knows how to access resources and assistance in developing and refining these skills	has some knowledge of how to access resources and assistance with techniques of representing and is willing, with support, to take risks and learn these skills	requires assistance to gain skills in representing through various media, and is open to receive such assistance	is dependent on external sources to identify and access support in gaining knowledge and skill in using media other than print to represent ideas and information
demonstrates ability to do independent revision and editing to improve the representation of information and ideas	demonstrates some ability to revise and edit, as well as a willingness to do so under guidance	requires external assessment and assistance to revise and edit representation of ideas and information	is unable and/or unwilling to edit or revise representations even when assistance or direction is given

Viewing Rubrics

Collect data for use with the viewing rubrics with the appropriate tools in the Assessment & Evaluation of Representing and Viewing section, and by observing student responses to what they "see" in terms of their questions and comments regarding films, television, games and visual texts. You can also use information gathered from formal testing of students' ability to respond to graphs, maps, pictures, diagrams, etc.

The student...

Highest Level			Lowest Level
Knowledge of Content			
is able to state the main purpose, impression or theme is able to retell or describe accurately the main elements and supporting detail, to make/understand inferences, and make sensible predictions and hypotheses	is able to tell the likely purpose of the presentation is able to retell or describe, with a fair degree of accuracy, the main elements and the supporting detail, to make/understand most inferences, and make sensible predictions	is able to speculate reasonably about the possible purpose of the presentation is able to retell or describe some main elements and supply some supporting detail; makes/understands few inferences, makes only some predictions	is not able to articulate the purpose of the presentation retells/describes a combination of main elements and details but without sequence or organization; is unable to make inferences or sensible predictions
Knowledge of Technique			
shows knowledge of techniques used to communicate the message/information	shows some knowledge of techniques used to communicate the message/information	shows knowledge, with prompting, of only the most obvious techniques used in the presentation	is not knowledgeable about technique and is unclear about the connection between technique and effect
Personal Response			
is able to respond personally to or relate to experience the elements of the presentation	is able to articulate personal response to the presentation	is able to say why he/she does or does not like the presentation	is unable to support his/her opinion of the presentation
Evaluation Skills			
is able to judge or criticize, against criteria, the effectiveness of the presentation	is able to give an opinion, supported by detail and example, about the effectiveness of the presentation	is able to say why he/she does or does not think the presentation is effective	is unable to judge whether or not the presentation is effective

SAMPLE TASK FOR ASSESSMENT OF VIEWING SKILLS

Have students view a non-print presentation. This could be a short documentary, a series of pictures, or a historical photograph. Visual products created by students (for example, posters, collages, computer projects) also work very well. (The assessment tools provided in the Representing and Viewing section can be used for students to evaluate the product.) **Explain the viewing rubric** to the students being assessed. **Ask the students questions** about the presentation. These can be oral or written, as suits the situation. The students' **responses to an evaluation instrument** will provide you with information about the last criterion in the rubric.

Critical Thinking

By using a wide range of information from all areas of student response (including informal interactions and formal assignments and texts), you can gain insight into students' cognitive abilities and collect data for use with the critical thinking rubrics. Any of the instruments in this book that deal with making comparisons, judging, assessing, speculating, hypothesizing, analyzing, or applying concepts can yield appropriate and applicable information.

The student...

Highest Level			Lowest Level
often asks insightful questions of a speculative nature	asks sensible and sometimes speculative questions	asks few questions, or primarily questions of a knowledge-based nature (Who? What?)	asks few or no questions, or primarily questions involving repetition of instructions
comments on and responds to written and oral questions, almost always showing a strong grasp of the concept presented	comments on and responds to written and oral questions, usually showing grasp of the concept presented	comments on and responds to written and oral questions, showing a weak or superficial grasp of the concept presented	does not volunteer comments, responds to written and oral questions only as required, usually showing little or no grasp of the concept presented
reliably represents the concept through analogies or comparisons	can often represent the concept through analogies or comparisons	needs assistance and support to represent the concept through analogies or comparisons	relies entirely on assistance and support from others to represent the concept through analogies or comparisons
easily supplies particular examples of applications of the concept	can usually supply an example of an application of the concept	supplies memorized examples of applications of the concept	cannot supply examples of applications of the concept
demonstrates, through representations, understanding of inferences and implications associated with the concept	demonstrates, through representations, understanding of some inferences and implications associated with the concept	has difficulty understanding (without coaching) inferences and implications associated with the concept	seldom understands inferences and implications associated with the concepts studied
can make sound judgments showing comprehension of the concept presented	can make judgments showing basic comprehension of the concept presented	makes faulty or illogical judgments (based on comprehension) of the concept presented	makes judgments unwillingly and is not able to show the reasoning behind these judgments as having any base in comprehension of the concept presented

Conducting Research

Collect data for use with the research rubrics by using information from the research-related tools in the Assessment & Evaluation of Representing and Viewing section, from observing student independence and level of confidence in seeking out information, and from student projects.

The student...

Highest Level			Lowest Level
Planning			
is able to define purpose clearly before beginning research	is able to define purpose before beginning research	with assistance, can define purpose before beginning research	knows the topic of intended research, but needs much assistance to define purpose
identifies audience and generates several appropriate possibilities for form/format of presentation	names audience and generates one or more appropriate possibilities for form/format of presentation	needs help to identify audience and generate appropriate form/format of presentation	needs help identifying audience and an appropriate form/format of presentation
Gathering Information			
knowledge of many sources of information, including non-print media, people, electronic sources, etc.	knowledge of some sources of information	knowledge of few sources of information apart from the obvious and traditional	knowledge of only the most obvious and traditional sources
ingenuity and confidence in searching out further sources	willingness to search out further sources	little interest/confidence in searching out further sources	little interest/confidence in searching out further sources
awareness of primary and secondary sources	some awareness of primary vs. secondary sources	does not distinguish between primary and secondary sources	does not distinguish between primary and secondary sources
able to generate questions that focus the scope of investigation	able to generate questions relevant to the investigation	difficulty generating questions to guide investigation	unable to generate useful questions to guide investigation
excellent book knowledge for efficient use of indices, tables of content, headings, visuals, etc.	enough book knowledge for a relatively efficient use of indices, table of contents, headings, visuals, etc.	too limited knowledge of book parts to make an efficient search	too limited knowledge of book parts to make an efficient search
proficient reading skills for skimming and scanning, and locating key words	reading skills for skimming, scanning, locating key words	little understanding of reading strategies for searching, so becomes overwhelmed trying to read everything word-for-word	no real reading strategies for searching, so is overwhelmed trying to read everything word-for-word

(continued...)

Gathering Information *(continued)*

competence in selection of relevant data, note-taking, recording of pertinent publishing information	fair competence in selection of relevant data, note taking, recording of pertinent publishing information	no real strategies for sorting and selecting relevant data	no real strategies for sorting and selecting relevant data
diverse skills, i.e. sketching, diagramming and charting to record	use of some skills, apart from writing, to record	weak note-taking skills or other skills for recording	no strategies for recording, apart from word-for-word copying of material

Final Product

includes excellent, relevant, accurate information successfully achieving the purpose of the investigation	includes sufficient, relevant, accurate information aligned with the purpose of the investigation	includes a minimum of relevant and accurate information, some of which is not aligned with the purpose of the investigation	includes insufficient information, some of which is irrelevant or not aligned with the purpose of the investigation
is sophisticated in the use of language and convention, well-organized and neat	is competent in the use of language and convention, well-organized and neat	is poorly organized, lacking in neatness and competence in the use of language and convention	is lacking in organization, in competence in the use of language, convention and general neatness
has an appropriate format, tone and style for the audience	has an appropriate format, tone and style for the audience	has uninteresting format, or one not suited in tone or style for the intended audience	has uninteresting format, or one not suited in tone or style for the intended audience
is imaginative and original			

Student-Created Rubrics

As a way of involving students in evaluation, have them help to create rubrics. For example, you might have them collaborate in creating the rubrics for evaluating a title page for a book. (It's best to start out with something that is this specific and limited in scope.) Explain to students that in order to create a rubric, one considers first what is being evaluated. Then, take students through the following steps. (Students may respond individually, in groups, or as a class. Write their responses on the board.)

✭ Have students analyze title pages of students from another class or of former students.

✭ Ask students:

   What is our current assigned project?

   What will we have when we are finished if we have done what we are asked to do?

✭ Suggest that they consider the following:

   Now that we have written down what it is we are aiming to accomplish, we need to imagine what the best possible title page would be.

   What information would it contain and how would it look? (They may want to include categories of Content, Artwork, and Conventions, among others.)

   How will we conclude that one title page is better than another?

   What are all the ways in which one product could be better than another?

   Look at each aspect of the assignment (listed on the board) to describe how it can be "great."

   In groups or partners, brainstorm as many possible ways in which a "good" project and a "great" project would be different. List them this way:

      A great project would be…

      A great project would have…

      A great project could include…

✭ List all of the groups' descriptors and ask students to identify those which can be combined or eliminated to reduce the list to essentials.

✭ Next, ask students to come up with descriptors that are the opposite (in terms of quantity and quality) of those on the list. Write the opposites next to the appropriate descriptors on the original list.

✭ Finally, have students supply two sets of descriptors that would describe products that fall between the extremes of each of the criteria. (This will be the most difficult task and will require your assistance.)

✭ You should create a final revised form and hand out to students as the criteria for evaluating a title page. When the projects are completed, students might be invited to evaluate their own project using the rubrics and to discuss how and why their evaluation differs, if it does, from yours.

NOTE: A blank form is provided on page 159.

75 Language Arts Assessment Tools • Scholastic Teaching Resources

Creating a Rubric
Create a General Rubric

When you are creating general rubrics, think about the changes that may occur *over time* and *across a variety of student responses* (e.g., student comments in discussion, questions asked, written work, exam answers, assignments).

Some of the following verbs are useful:

demonstrates	represents	generates	selects
writes	considers	contributes	participates
listens	responds	applies	
speaks	produces	collaborates	
shows	uses	reads	

Some of the following competence qualifiers are suitable...

At the *highest level of competence:*

often	evident	predictably	level
many	thoughtful	well-developed	varied
strong	consistently	purposeful	independently
clear	most	complete	excellent
always	sophisticated	frequently	articulate
several	insightful	competent	

At the *second level of competence:*

usually	at times	good	some
competent	often	on occasion	
satisfactory	suitable	adequate	

At the *third level of competence:*

only with assistance	unclear	unsupported by	disorganized
basic	undeveloped	fair	generalized
incomplete	inaccurate	weak	
irrelevant	seldom	evidence or example	
with support	imprecise	inconsistent	

At the *lowest level of competence:*

weak	off topic	incomplete
lacking in organization	shows little knowledge of	muddled
little evidence of	student is unable to	has limited skill with
even with assistance	undeveloped	
not evident	unsatisfactory	

Creating a Rubric
Create a Specific Rubric

Begin creating specific rubrics by imagining the best possible performance or product of the type you are evaluating.

Ask yourself:

What would its content include?
Think about amount and quality of information.

What would its form or structure be like?
Think about organization, accuracy of form, sophistication of form.

How would the level of language and style be described?
Think about terminology, vocabulary, voice, tone.

What would characterize the final product or performance?
Think about uniqueness, originality, polish, presentation.

NOTE: A blank rubric form is provided on page 159.

Rubric Form

The student...

Highest Level			Lowest Level

PROFESSIONAL RESOURCES

Authentic Reading Assessment: Practices and Possibilities, S. Valencia. Newark, DE: International Reading Association, 1993.

Evaluating Literacy: A Perspective for Change, R.J. Anthony. Portsmouth, NH: Heinemann Educational Books, 1991.

Language Across the Curriculum: Teaching Children to Be Literate, V. Froese. Toronto, Ontario: Harcourt Brace Canada, 1997.

Literacy Assessment: A Handbook of Instruments, L.K. Rhodes, ed. Portsmouth, NH: Heinemann Educational Books, 1993.

Literature Circles and Response, B. Campbell Hill. Norwood, MA: Christopher-Gordon Publishers, 1995.

Observing Young Readers, M. Clay. Auckland, New Zealand: Heinemann, 1982.

Portfolio Assessment: Getting Started, A. De Fina. New York, NY: Scholastic Inc., 1992.

Portfolio Assessment in the Reading-Writing Classroom, R. Tierney, M. Carter, and L. Desai. Norwood, MA: Christopher-Gordon Publishers, 1991.

Portfolios in the Classroom, J. Clemmons, L. Laase, D. Cooper, N. Areglado, and M. Dill. New York, NY: Scholastic Inc., 1993.

Practical Aspects of Authentic Assessment: Putting the Pieces Together, B. Campbell Hill and C. Ruptic. Toronto, Ontario: Irwin Publishing, 1994.

Practical Assessments for Literature-Based Reading Classrooms, A Fiderer. New York, NY: Scholastic Inc., 1992.

Reading Assessments in Practice, K. Ransom. Newark, DE: International Reading Association, 1995.

Reading Instruction That Makes Sense, M. Tarasoff. Victoria, British Columbia: Active Learning Institute, 1993.

Retelling, Relating, Reflecting Beyond the 3 Rs, S. Schwartz and M. Bone. Concord, Ontario: Irwin Publishing,1995.

Setting and Using Criteria, K. Gregory, C. Cameron, and A. Davies. Mervill, British Columbia: Connections Publishing, 1997.

Standards for the Assessment of Reading and Writing, International Reading Association and National Council of Teachers of English. Newark, DE: International Reading Association, 1994.

Teaching Children to Read and Write, Scarborough Board of Education. Scarborough, Ontario: Scarborough Board, 1997.

Windows into Literacy: Assessing Learners K-8, L.K. Rhodes. Portsmouth, NH: Heinemann Educational Books, 1993.